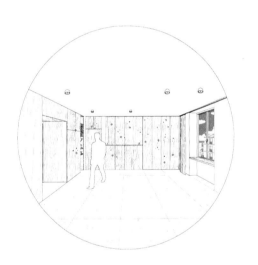

booq
publishing

© 2017 **booq** publishing, S.L.
c/ Domènech, 7-9, 2º 1ª
08012 Barcelona, Spain

ISBN 978-84-945662-9-5 [EN]
ISBN 978-84-945662-6-4 [DE]

Derechos de publicación y distribución
en lengua española en propiedad de:

© 2017 EDITORS S.A.
C/ Horts d'en Mateu
Pol. Industrial Sur
08450 Llinars del Vallès
Barcelona, España

Telf. +34 938 410 351
iberlibro@iberlibroediciones.com
www.iberlibroediciones.com

ISBN 978-84-459-0934-8 [ES]

Editorial coordination:
Claudia Martínez Alonso

Art direction:
Mireia Casanovas Soley

Edition:
Francesc Zamora Mola

Translation:
Thinking Abroad

Printed in Spain

006	INTRODUCTION	176	THE GRID
008	PIVOT APARTMENT	184	VILLA INTERIOR
024	BRERA APARTMENT	192	WORKROOM ARCHITECTS
034	SMALL HOME, SMART HOME	202	PENTHOUSE V
042	FLAT 8	208	STEEL STOOL
050	NANLUOGUXIANG HUTONG	210	STABLE IN WEST FLANDERS
060	DENGSHIKOU HUTONG RESIDENCE	218	APARTMENT V01
074	BUILDING WARDROBE	228	INHABITED WOODEN WALLS
078	QUATRE SEPTEMBRE APARTMENT	234	LYNKO NOMADIC FURNITURE SYSTEM
086	BRANDBURG HOME AND STUDIO	242	TERRACED HOUSE
092	ART COLLECTOR'S LOFT	248	WEISEL APARTMENT
100	ART STORAGE	254	LONG ESTATE
106	NEST SHELF	260	PETER'S APARTMENT
108	TOY MANAGEMENT HOUSE	268	MY HOME AND OFFICE
118	FERMI	274	EAST COAST APARTMENT
126	STUDIO FLAT	284	VIVID COLOR
134	KOWLOON BAY	294	PINORAMA
140	A GRAPHIC REFURBISHMENT BY THE SEA	298	M HOUSE
148	THE STUDIO	306	LIVING SPACE
152	KERAMOS	312	MOORMANN'S KAMMERSPIEL
156	LEVENT HOUSE	322	ISLINGTON MAISONETTE
166	MODULOR	330	VITRINA COLLECTION AND WARDROBE SYSTEM

It shouldn't come as a surprise if you hear that it is the integration of storage solutions that really rounds off a good home design. With no doubt, it is a crucial design element that requires great attention to detail. All the fantastic ideas featured in the book are at the top of their game. The book features creative storage solutions for every room in the house. Storage units can fold, nest and collapse for easy handling, storage can double duty to conserve valuable floor area. Open or closed, built-in or freestanding, storage possibilities are endless, but most importantly should be tailored to our needs and to the items to be put away or displayed.

As some of the featured projects demonstrate, storage is most efficient when it is tailored to the habits of the users and to the items to be stored away and organized.

Organization goes hand in hand with storage. It facilitates immediate access to the items we are looking for, and saves us time and frustration. It also seems obvious that the most ingenious storage ideas for the home appear to be those that make best use of the available space.

It is safe to say that built-ins are the most efficient solution when it comes to saving floor space. The need for freestanding furniture is minimized, and valuable floor space is cleared for one's enjoyment.

When it comes to choosing between open and closed storage, it is just a matter of taste and practicality. Storage can conceal or display, and most often, homes have a mix of both. But as mentioned earlier, storage is most efficient when it is tailored to the items to be stored away. For instance, in a kitchen, open shelving and closed storage are common. Open shelving or niches can highlight special tableware, or can contain utensils that are frequently used; on the other hand, anything can go into closed cabinets, neatly stored out of sight.

Small spaces are perhaps more apt to trigger the most creative ideas. Size matters, and ingenious storage ideas are most needed in tight spaces.

Looking on the bright side, while the lack of storage space can be a nightmare for small home dwellers, they can also be an opportunity for the uncovering of mind-blowing design opportunities.

Dass das Einbinden von Stauraumlösungen eine gute Heimgestaltung erst richtig abrundet, sollte keine Überraschung darstellen. Zweifellos ist es ein entscheidendes Designelement, das große Liebe zum Detail erfordert. All die fantastischen Ideen, die in diesem Buch beschrieben werden, sind die besten zu diesem Thema. Das Buch präsentiert kreative Stauraumlösungen für jeden Raum im Haus. Für eine einfache Handhabung lassen sich Stauraumlösungen falten, verschachteln und zusammenklappen und übernehmen dabei eine Doppelfunktion, um wertvolle Bodenfläche einzusparen. Offen oder geschlossen, eingebaut oder freistehend, sind Aufbewahrungsmöglichkeiten schier endlos: Was jedoch am wichtigsten ist: Sie sollten auf unsere Bedürfnisse und die Elemente, die aufgeräumt oder gezeigt werden sollen, zugeschnitten sein.

Wie einige der vorgestellten Projekte zeigen, ist Aufbewahrung am effizientesten, wenn sie auf die Gewohnheiten der Benutzer und Elemente zugeschnitten ist, die verstaut und geordnet werden sollen.

Ordnung geht Hand in Hand mit Aufbewahrung. Sie ermöglicht den sofortigen Zugang zu Elementen, die wir suchen, und spart dadurch Zeit und erspart uns Frustration. Einleuchtend ist ebenso, dass die genialsten Aufbewahrungsideen für das Haus anscheinend diejenigen sind, die den vorhandenen Raum am besten nutzen.

Es lässt sich mit Sicherheit behaupten, dass Einbauten die effizienteste Lösung sind, wenn es darum geht, Platz zu sparen. Der Bedarf an freistehenden Möbeln wird minimiert und wertvolle Nutzfläche wird für den eigenen Genuss geräumt.

Die Entscheidung für eine offene und geschlossene Aufbewahrung ist allein eine Frage des Geschmacks und der Umsetzbarkeit. Die Art der Aufbewahrung kann Dinge verbergen oder zeigen, und häufig haben Wohnstätten eine Mischung aus beidem. Doch wie zuvor bereits erwähnt, ist die Aufbewahrung am effizientesten, wenn sie auf die Elemente, die verstaut werden sollten, zugeschnitten ist. In einer Küche beispielsweise sind offene Regale und eine geschlossene Aufbewahrung üblich. Offene Regale oder Nischen können ein besonderes Geschirr hervorheben oder Geräte enthalten, die häufig verwendet werden; andererseits kann alles fein säuberlich und nicht einsehbar in geschlossenen Schränken lagern.

Möglicherweise eignen sich kleine Räume eher dazu, die kreativsten Ideen hervorzubringen. Es kommt auf die Größe an, und geniale Stauraumideen sind in engen Räumen dringend erforderlich.

Während der Mangel an Speicherplatz ein Alptraum für die Bewohner kleiner Wohnstätten sein kann, kann er, positiv betrachtet, auch eine Chance sein, überwältigende Gestaltungschancen zu entdecken.

L'organisation du rangement occupe une place toute particulière dans la réussite d'une architecture d'intérieur bien conçue et requiert de porter une grande attention aux détails. Les idées inventives proposées dans ce livre offrent des choix très efficaces et créatifs pour chaque pièce de la maison. Des modules de rangement, notamment, peuvent se plier, s'encastrer ou basculer pour être faciles à manipuler, ou encore faire double usage afin de préserver un précieux espace au sol.

Qu'elles soient ouvertes ou fermées, intégrées ou autonomes, les solutions sont infinies et se doivent d'être adaptées à nos besoins et aux objets, selon que l'on souhaite les ranger ou les exposer.

Comme le montrent les projets rassemblés ici, le rangement est plus efficace lorsqu'il est adapté aux habitudes des usagers et prévu en fonction des éléments à ranger et à organiser.

L'organisation va de pair avec le rangement. Elle facilite l'accès immédiat aux objets recherchés, et nous épargne temps perdu et frustration. Il semble également évident que les idées de rangement les plus ingénieuses pour la maison sont celles qui utilisent de façon optimale l'espace disponible.

On peut dire sans hésiter que les solutions incorporées sont les plus efficaces pour économiser de l'espace au sol. Le besoin de mobilier autonome est réduit, et la surface est dégagée pour le plaisir de tous.

Mais le choix du rangement ouvert ou fermé répond aussi à une question de goût et de praticité. Les maisons comportent généralement les deux options à la fois. Par exemple, dans une cuisine, il est commun de trouver des étagères et des placards fermés. Les rayonnages ou les niches peuvent mettre en valeur un service de table spécial ou peuvent contenir des ustensiles d'usage fréquent.

Les petits espaces sont peut-être les plus aptes à inciter aux idées les plus créatives et si le manque d'espace de rangement peut s'avérer un véritable cauchemar pour les propriétaires de logement aux dimensions réduites, il représente également une chance de découvrir des opportunités d'aménagement extraordinaires.

No debemos sorprendernos si escuchamos que la integración de soluciones de almacenamiento es la que realmente pone la guinda al diseño de una vivienda. Sin duda, es un elemento de diseño crucial que necesita de mucho detalle. Y en este ejemplar hemos reunidos las ideas más destacadas en su campo. En las próximas páginas se desarrollan soluciones de almacenamiento creativas para cada estancia de la vivienda. Las unidades de almacenaje pueden doblarse, anidarse y contraerse para facilitar su manipulación. Además de guardar, las soluciones de almacenamiento sirven para mantener libre el espacio. Abierto o cerrado, integrado o independiente, las posibilidades de almacenaje son infinitas, pero lo más importante es que se adapten a nuestras necesidades y a los objetos que deben guardar o mostrar.

Como muestran algunos de los proyectos destacados, el almacenamiento es más eficiente cuando se personaliza a los hábitos de los habitantes y a los objetos que deben guardarse o mostrarse.

La organización va de la mano con el almacenamiento. Facilita el acceso inmediato a los objetos que buscamos, nos ahorra tiempo y frustración. Parece también obvio que las ideas de almacenamiento más ingeniosas para el hogar son aquellas que hacen un uso intensivo del espacio disponible.

Podemos añadir que los muebles integrados son la solución más eficiente cuando se trata de ahorrar espacio. La necesidad de mobiliario independiente se minimiza y el apreciado espacio se libera para nuestro disfrute.

Cuando se trata de elegir entre almacenaje abierto o cerrado, es simplemente un tema de gusto y practicidad. El almacenamiento puede ocultar o mostrar, y normalmente, las viviendas tienen una mezcla de los dos. Pero, como mencionamos antes, el almacenamiento es más eficiente cuando se personaliza para los objetos que deben guardarse o mostrarse. Por ejemplo, es común ver en una cocina estanterías abiertas y almacenamiento cerrado. Las estanterías abiertas o nichos pueden destacar objetos especiales de la vajilla o contener utensilios que son muy usados. Por otro lado, cualquier cosa puede guardarse ordenadamente en un armario cerrado, para no ser vista.

Los espacios pequeños tal vez sean más aptos para provocar las ideas más creativas. El tamaño importa y las ideas de almacenamiento más ingeniosas son más necesarias en espacios reducidos.

Mirando el lado positivo, aunque la falta de espacio de almacenamiento puede ser una pesadilla para los habitantes de viviendas pequeñas, también puede ser una oportunidad para desvelar increíbles oportunidades de diseño.

37 m² // 400 sq ft

Photo © Robert Garneau

PIVOT APARTMENT // ARCHITECTURE WORKSHOP PC

NEW YORK, NEW YORK, UNITED STATES

Pivot is a pre-war studio transformed into an adaptable space. The brief called for a design that would make this space suitable for entertaining. Inspired by a Swiss army knife, the space is conceived as an object that expands to reveal different functions.

Pivot ist ein Studio aus der Vorkriegszeit, das in einen anpassungsfähigen Raum umgewandelt wurde. Die Vorgabe verlangte ein Design, das diesen Raum für den Empfang von Gästen geeignet machen würde. In Anlehnung an ein Schweizer Armeemesser wird der Raum als Gegenstand begriffen, der sich ausdehnt, um verschiedene Funktionen zu entfalten.

Pivot est un studio d'avant-guerre transformé en espace modulable. L'énoncé du projet prévoyait de concevoir un espace adapté afin d'accueillir les invités. Inspiré des multiples fonctionnalités du couteau suisse, l'espace est conçu pour révéler leur éventail de possibilités.

Pivot es un estudio de antes de la guerra transformado en espacio flexible. El objetivo del diseño era crear un espacio que fuera adecuado para recibir visitas. Inspirado en una navaja suiza, el espacio se concibe como un objeto que se expande para ofrecer diferentes funciones.

www.aw-pc.com // Team: Robert Garneau and Eric Ansel

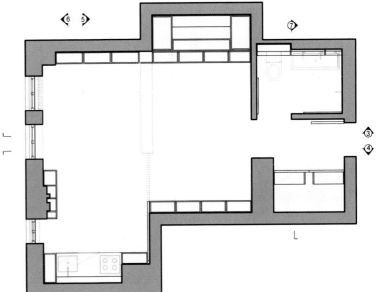

Floor plan

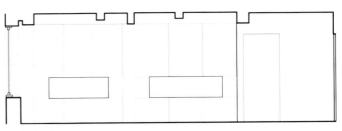

North elevation

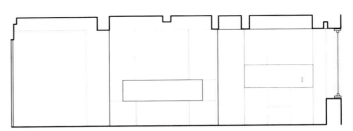

South elevation

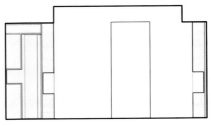

East elevation

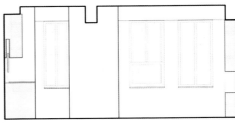

West elevation

The design of the apartment emphasizes the openness and multi-functionality of the space. It is fit to accommodate ten for dinner, six for sleeping, a home office, a private study, and an efficient kitchen for a client who loves to entertain.

Die Gestaltung der Wohnung unterstreicht die Offenheit und Multifunktionalität des Raumes. Dort können 10 Personen zu Abend essen und sechs Personen übernachten, ein Homeoffice, eine eigener Arbeitsraum und eine effiziente Küche für einen Kunden, der gerne Gäste bewirtet.

La conception de cet appartement souligne l'ouverture et la multifonctionnalité de l'espace. L'appartement permet d'accueillir dix personnes à dîner et six pour dormir, il dispose d'un bureau à domicile, d'un cabinet privé et d'une cuisine équipée pour toutes les personnes qui aiment recevoir.

El diseño del apartamento enfatiza la amplitud y multifuncionalidad del espacio. Puede acoger a diez personas para cenar, seis para dormir, un despacho, un estudio y una cocina eficiente para un cliente al que le gusta recibir invitados.

The kitchen features a backsplash that lifts to reveal storage behind. An expanding hydraulic table can be used for work or can extend into the main space when hosting guests for dinner. It can also rise up at the push of a button for additional kitchen counter space.

Die Küche hat einen Fliesenspiegel, der sich anheben lässt, um Stauraum freizulegen. Ein erweiterbarer hydraulischer Tisch kann zum Arbeiten genutzt werden oder sich in den Hauptraum ausbreiten, wenn Gäste zum Abendessen kommen. Auf Knopfdruck kann er auch nach oben gefahren werden, so dass eine zusätzliche Küchenarbeitsfläche entsteht.

La cuisine présente un dosseret qu'il suffit de soulever pour découvrir l'espace de rangement dissimulé derrière. Une table hydraulique extensible peut servir de bureau de travail ou se prolonger dans l'espace de vie pour accueillir vos invités autour d'un dîner. Vous pouvez aussi la surélever en appuyant simplement sur un bouton afin de disposer d'un plan de travail plus important dans la cuisine.

La cocina tiene una placa en el frontal de la pared, que se eleva para mostrar un espacio de almacenaje. La mesa extensible, con altura regulable, se puede utilizar para trabajar o para ampliar el espacio principal en caso de tener invitados para cenar. O incluso, pulsando el botón, puede ser una encimera adicional de la cocina.

Residents come home to an airy modern apartment, where everything comfortably has its place. This is achieved through a wide range of multifunctional design elements that make the most of the available space, while offering creative and efficient storage solutions.

Die Bewohner kommen nach Hause in eine luftige moderne Wohnung, in der alles bequem seinen Platz hat. Dies wird durch eine große Auswahl an multifunktionellen Designelementen erzielt, die aus dem vorhandenen Raum das Beste machen und gleichzeitig kreative und effiziente Lösungen in Sachen Stauraum bieten.

Les occupants entrent chez eux dans un appartement moderne et spacieux où tout objet trouve aisément sa place. Tel est le résultat d'un ensemble d'éléments multifonctionnels qui maximise l'espace disponible, tout en servant de systèmes de rangement ingénieux et pratiques.

A su llegada, los habitantes de la casa se encuentran un apartamento moderno y espacioso, donde prima el confort. Este efecto se ha logrado utilizando un amplio abanico de elementos de diseño multifuncionales que aprovechan al máximo el espacio disponible, a la vez que ofrecen soluciones de almacenaje creativas y eficientes.

The resident can dramatically alter the space to support different functional needs. While very appealing, this notion represented an important challenge: the option to transform the space at any given time meant that the various configurations of the space had to be coordinated with just as varied storage possibilities.

Der Bewohner kann den Raum nachdrücklich verändern, so dass er unterschiedliche Anforderungen an die Funktion erfüllt. Diese Idee war zwar sehr ansprechend und stellte eine wichtige Herausforderung dar: Die Möglichkeit, den Raum zu jedem beliebigen Zeitpunkt umzugestalten, bedeutete, dass die verschiedenen Anordnungen des Raumes mit ebenso vielfältigen Stauraummöglichkeiten koordiniert werden mussten.

Le résident peut modifier entièrement l'espace au gré de ses différents besoins. Ce concept, avec tous ses attraits, présentait cependant un défi important : chaque transformation dans l'agencement de l'espace devait conserver, à tout moment, autant d'options de rangement.

El habitante puede modificar el espacio para diferentes necesidades funcionales. Aunque era muy atractivo, este hecho representaba un reto importante: la opción de transformar el espacio en cualquier momento significaba que sus diversas configuraciones tenían que coordinarse con opciones de almacenamiento muy variadas.

A pivoting wall cabinet divides the apartment in two, where either space can be used independently when needed, revealing a wall-bed with an operable window-niche.

Ein schwenkbarer Wandschrank gliedert die Wohnung in zwei Bereiche, die bei Bedarf unabhängig voneinander genutzt werden können, hierbei wird ein Schrankbett mit einer funktionellen Fensternische sichtbar.

La paroi du cabinet pivote, divisant ainsi l'appartement en deux espaces pouvant être utilisés indépendamment au besoin. Un lit-armoire apparaît alors avec une fenêtre à ouverture modulable encastrée dans une niche.

El armario de pared pivotante divide el apartamento en dos y deja a la vista una cama abatible. Este también dispone de una abertura que deja pasar la luz natural permitiendo el uso del espacio de forma independiente si fuera necesario.

The sleeping area is fitted with closets on two sides. They are equipped with pull-down rods, shelves and drawers, offering different compact, yet organized storage options for all type of garments and accessories.

Der Schlafbereich ist an zwei Seiten mit Wandschränken ausgestattet. Sie sind mit ausziehbaren Stangen, Regalen und Fächern ausgestattet, die verschiedene kompakte und dennoch organisierte Stauraumoptionen für Kleidungsstücke und Accessoires aller Art bieten.

L'espace chambre dispose de deux placards latéraux équipés de barres extensibles, d'étagères et de tiroirs, offrant différentes possibilités de rangement compactes correspondant à tout genre de vêtements ou accessoires.

La zona de descanso está equipada con armarios a ambos lados con barras deslizantes, estantes y cajones, que ofrecen diversas alternativas de almacenaje para todo tipo de prendas y accesorios.

The bathroom appears sleek and clutter-free thanks to a minimal design featuring a large curbless shower that allows for continuous flooring, hence making the bathroom look larger. All the bathroom supplies are hidden within a large medicine cabinet with mirror doors and integrated lighting.

Das Badezimmer wirkt gepflegt und übersichtlich dank des minimalen Designs mit einer großen randlosen Dusche, die einen durchgängigen Bodenbelag ermöglicht und das Bad folglich größer erscheinen lässt. Alle Badezimmerutensilien sind in einem großen Arzneischrank mit Spiegeltüren und integrierter Beleuchtung verborgen.

La salle de bains est stylée et dégagée grâce à son design minimaliste qui présente une grande douche sans bordures et dont le revêtement au sol est continu, donnant ainsi à la pièce une impression de largeur importante. Tous les meubles sont dissimulés derrière une grande armoire à pharmacie avec des portes miroir et un éclairage intégré.

El diseño minimalista del baño le aporta elegancia y orden. Destaca la gran zona de ducha sin bordillo que permite la continuidad del pavimento, lo que le da una sensación de mayor amplitud. Todos los artículos de aseo están ocultos en un gran armario de baño con puertas de espejo y luz integrada.

The entrance closet doors have built-in shelving for hats and shoes as well as a hanging rod that lights up when the door is opened.

Die Türen des Wandschranks am Eingang haben eingebaute Fächer für Hüte und Schuhe sowie eine Kleiderstange, die beleuchtet wird, wenn die Tür geöffnet wird.

Les portes du placard d'entrée sont assorties d'étagères intégrées pour les chapeaux et les chaussures, ainsi qu'une penderie qui s'éclaire à l'ouverture de la porte.

Las puertas del armario de la entrada tienen estantes para sombreros y zapatos así como una barra para colgar prendas que se ilumina cuando se abre la puerta.

34 m² // 366 sq ft

Photo © Luca Broglia

BRERA APARTMENT // CESARE GALLIGANI, PLANAIR

MILAN, ITALY

The design for this apartment is characterized by a flexible layout achieved by means of a series of moving partitions, which can alter the configuration of the space and provide for a multitude of storage possibilities, including cupboards, drawers, cubbies, and shelves, making the most of every nook and cranny.

Der Entwurf für diese Wohnung ist durch einen flexiblen Grundriss gekennzeichnet, der mithilfe einer Reihe beweglicher Trennwände erzielt wird, welche die Ausgestaltung des Raumes verändern und eine Menge Stauraummöglichkeiten, darunter Schränke, Fächer, CGläserablagen und Regale bereitstellen können und somit aus jedem Winkel das Beste machen.

L'agencement de cet appartement se caractérise par une série de cloisons mobiles qui permettent de modifier la configuration de l'espace et offrent une multitude de possibilités de rangement, comprenant des placards, des tiroirs, des étagères, des coffres s'agençant dans chaque petit recoin.

El diseño de este apartamento se caracteriza por tener una distribución flexible del espacio, lograda mediante una serie de particiones móviles, que pueden modificar su configuración y brindar una multitud de posibilidades de almacenaje, incluyendo armarios, cajones, pequeños espacios y estantes, aprovechando al máximo cada rincón.

www.planairstudio.com // Team: Danilo Monzani, Mert Bokurt, and Andrea Zammataro

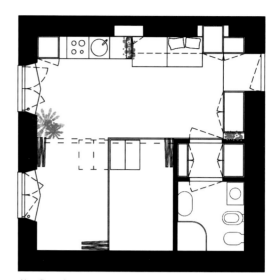
New floor plan

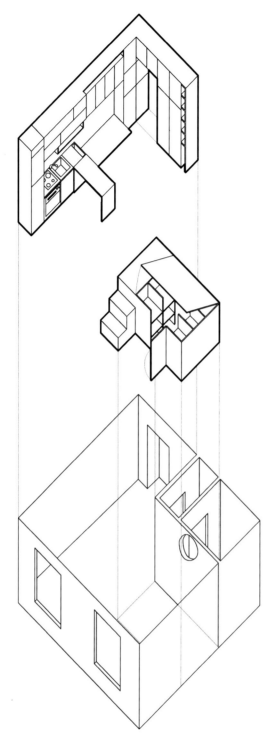
Exploded axonometric

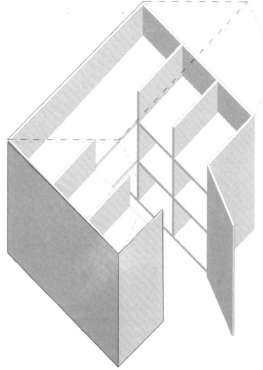
Bed wardrobe axonometric view

The functions of the space are organized along the living room's perimeter without blocking the light from two large windows. The use of space is optimized thanks to compact functional elements, freeing the space as much as possible, and exposing it to the light.

Die Funktionen des Raumes werden entlang der Wohnzimmerumlauflinie angeordnet, ohne das durch zwei große Fenster einfallende Licht zu behindern. Die Raumnutzung wird dank der kompakten Funktionselemente optimiert, die so viel Raum wie möglich freigeben und dem Licht aussetzen.

Les différentes fonctionnalités de l'espace sont organisées tout le long du périmètre du séjour sans gêner la lumière pénétrant par les deux grandes fenêtres. L'utilisation de l'espace est optimisée grâce à des éléments fonctionnels compacts, ce qui libère le plus d'espace possible tout en l'exposant à la lumière.

Las funciones del espacio se organizan a lo largo del perímetro del salón sin bloquear la luz que entra por los dos grandes ventanales. El uso del espacio se optimiza gracias a elementos funcionales compactos, que lo liberan al máximo y lo dejan abierto a la luz.

PRIVACY

OPENNESS AND LIGHT

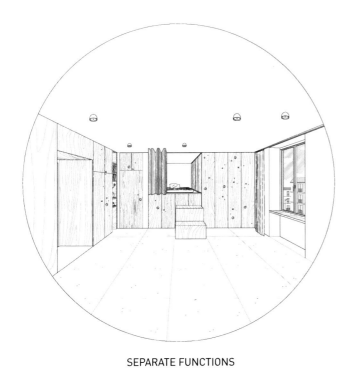

SEPARATE FUNCTIONS

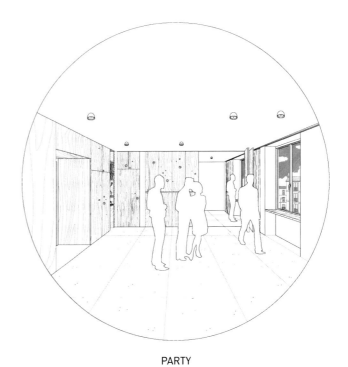

PARTY

Perspective views

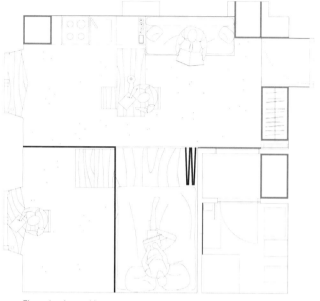

Floor plan for working

Floor plan for sleeping

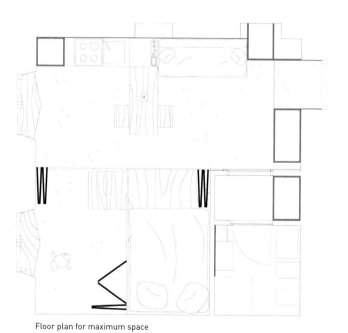

Floor plan for maximum space

Floor plan for entertainment

The interior is formally determined by integrated furniture able to encompass different functions and characteristics. The pieces of furniture act as spatial boundaries.

Der Innenbereich wird formal durch die integrierten Möbel bestimmt, die verschiedene Funktionen und Eigenschaften umfassen können. Die Möbelstücke dienen als räumliche Begrenzungen.

L'intérieur est simplement déterminé par les meubles intégrés qui réunissent différentes fonctions et caractéristiques. Les meubles délimitent les différents espaces.

El interior está formado por muebles integrados que permiten diferentes funciones y características. Los muebles actúan como límites espaciales.

The shapes of the different forms of storage are conceived based on the type of item they are to contain. Their positioning depends on how easily they need to be reached.

Die Form der verschiedenen Stauraumarten ist je nach Art des zu beherbergenden Elements konzipiert. Deren Positionierung hängt davon ab, wie leicht sie erreicht werden müssen.

Les différents rangements ont été conçus en fonction du type d'objet qu'ils doivent accueillir. Leur position dans la pièce dépend de leur nécessité à être facilement accessibles ou non.

Las diferentes formas de almacenaje han sido concebidas según los objetos que contienen. Su ubicación depende de la necesidad o no de tener a mano dichos objetos.

The design capitalises on high-impact ideas, whether is views through a peephole, or surfaces that partially fold away to reveal parts of the apartment.

Der Entwurf setzt auf Ideen mit starker Wirkung, wie etwa ein Guckloch oder Flächen, die sich teilweise zusammenklappen lassen, um Teile der Wohnung zu enthüllen.

Le concept de l'appartement est des plus innovants : certaines parties sont visibles aux travers de petites ouvertures puis se dévoilent au gré des modulations des parois.

El diseño saca el máximo rendimiento a ideas de gran impacto, ya sea produciendo el efecto de mirar a través de una mirilla o creando superficies que se pliegan parcialmente para dejar ver zonas del apartamento.

29 m² // 309 sq ft

Photo © Sottage Visual and LAAB

SMALL HOME, SMART HOME // LAAB

HONG LONG, SAR CHINA

This small apartment makes the most of the limited space without sacrificing comfort.
The owners' wish list for the renovation of their apartment included a full kitchen, a bathtub, a home cinema, a gym, and plenty of storage space. The owners also requested that the space be pet-friendly.

Diese kleine Wohnung macht das Beste aus dem begrenzten Platz, ohne dabei Komfort einzubüßen.
Auf der Wunschliste der Bewohner für die Renovierung ihrer Wohnung standen eine vollausgestattete Küche, eine Badewanne, ein Heimkino, ein Fitnessraum und sehr viel Stauraum. Die Inhaber wünschten sich zudem, dass der Raum haustierfreundlich sein sollte.

Ce petit appartement tire parti de l'espace limité sans sacrifier le confort de vie.
Sur la liste des souhaits du propriétaire pour la rénovation de son appartement, il y avait : une cuisine équipée, une baignoire, un home cinéma, une salle de gym, et beaucoup de rangements. Les occupants voulaient également que l'espace soit adapté aux animaux.

Este pequeño apartamento aprovecha al máximo su limitado espacio sin sacrificar la comodidad.
La lista de peticiones de los propietarios para la renovación de su apartamento incluía una cocina completa, una bañera, un cine en casa, un gimnasio y un montón de espacio de almacenamiento. Los propietarios también solicitaron que el espacio fuera apto para mascotas.

www.laab.pro // Team: Otto Ng, Ricci Wong, Yip Chun Hang, Kathy Li, Happy Yam, Zion Chan, Kenneth Cheung, Honley Cheuk, Jason Choi, Venus Kwok, Anthony Lee, Hugo Ma, Kinmo Ng, CK Wong, Sian Wong, and Phoebe Ng

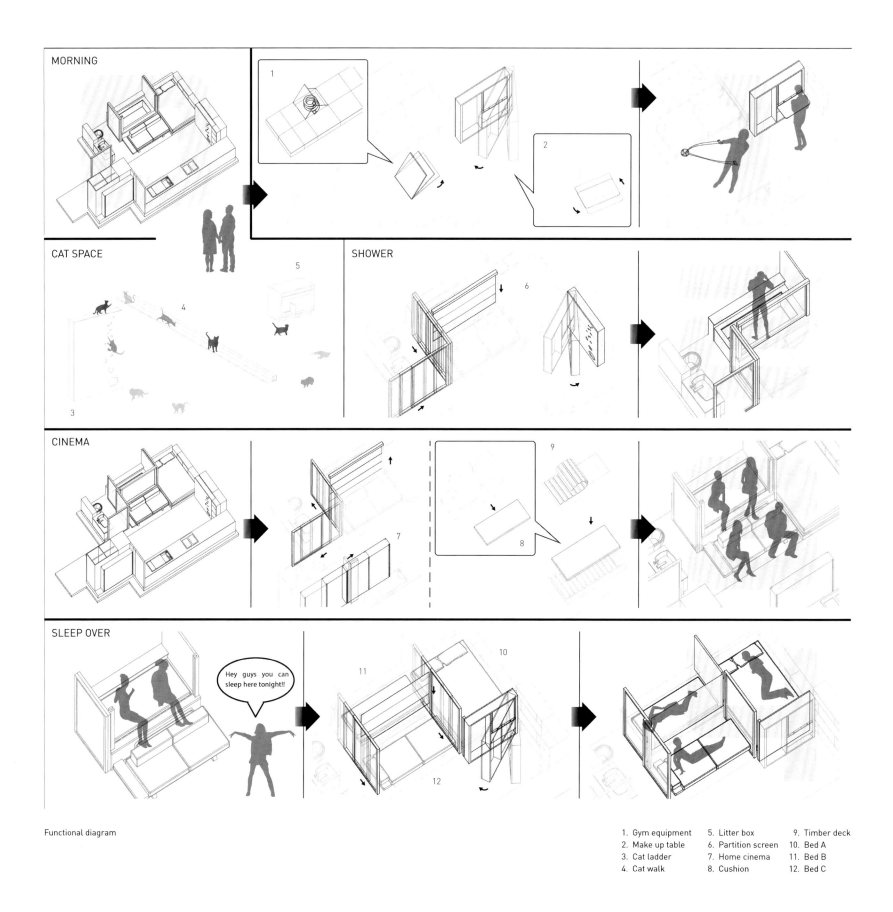

Functional diagram

1. Gym equipment
2. Make up table
3. Cat ladder
4. Cat walk
5. Litter box
6. Partition screen
7. Home cinema
8. Cushion
9. Timber deck
10. Bed A
11. Bed B
12. Bed C

According to the architects, the only way to achieve the goals was to incorporate multifunctional elements. Basically the small space had to transform itself to adapt to different situations.

Nach Ansicht der Architekten war der einzige Weg, diese Ziele zu erreichen, Multifunktionselemente einzubinden. Grundsätzlich musste sich der kleine Raum verwandeln, um sich an unterschiedliche Situationen anzupassen.

Selon les architectes, la seule façon d'atteindre ces objectifs était d'intégrer des modules multifonctionnels. En bref, il fallait que cet espace réduit puisse se transformer pour s'adapter à différentes situations.

Desde el punto de vista de los arquitectos, la única manera de lograr los objetivos pasaba por incorporar elementos multifuncionales. Básicamente, el pequeño espacio tenía que transformarse para adaptarse a diferentes situaciones.

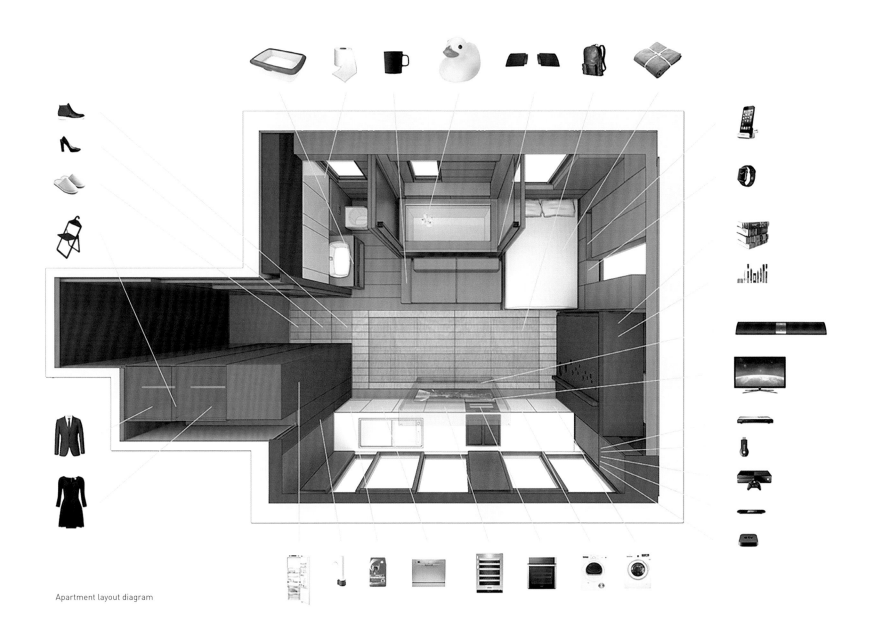

Apartment layout diagram

Flexible spaces and multi-functionality were key in the design of this small apartment. Meticulous planning and extraordinary craftsmanship was fundamental for the creation of this ultra-functional apartment. Detailing and mechanical systems were specially designed to maintain the apartment dry, clean and odourless.

Flexible Räume und Multifunktionalität waren der Schlüssel für die Gestaltung dieser kleinen Wohnung. Sorgfältige Planung und außerordentliches, handwerkliches Können waren bei der Gestaltung dieser extrem funktionalen Wohnung von grundlegender Bedeutung. Detaillierende und mechanische Systeme wurden eigens entworfen, um die Wohnung trocken, sauber und geruchlos zu halten.

Il était fondamental de créer des espaces modulables et multifonctionnels pour aménager ce petit appartement. Une planification méticuleuse et un savoir-faire extraordinaire étaient nécessaires pour répondre à ce défi. Des systèmes mécaniques ont été conçus spécialement pour que l'appartement reste sec, propre et sans odeur.

Los espacios flexibles y multifuncionales fueron la clave del diseño de este pequeño apartamento. Una planificación meticulosa y un extraordinario trabajo artesanal fueron los hilos conductores de la creación de este apartamento ultrafuncional. Se diseñaron unos sistemas mecánicos y concretos para mantener el apartamento seco, limpio y sin olor.

The bathtub area can turn into a comfortable raised platform behind and above the seating area, and can also serve as guestroom for short stays.

Der Badewannenbereich kann zu einer bequemen erhöhten Plattform hinter und über dem Sitzbereich werden und zudem als Gästezimmer für Kurzaufenthalte dienen.

Le coin baignoire peut être transformé en une confortable plateforme surélevée derrière et au-dessus du coin salon, et peut également servir de chambre d'amis pour de courts séjours.

La zona de la bañera se convierte en una cómoda plataforma elevada detrás y por encima de la zona de estar, que puede también servir como habitación de invitados para estancias cortas.

51 m² // 550 sq ft

Photo © Hazel Yuen Fun

FLAT 8 // DESIGN EIGHT FIVE TWO

HONG KONG, SAR CHINA

For Flat 8, the brief from the client was simple: to create a home as large as space and functions would allow, customized to suit the owners requirements. Windows and storage units are the main vertical surfaces interposed between the floor and the ceiling.

Für Wohnung 8 war die Anweisung des Kunden einfach: Ein Heim so groß, wie es Raum und Funktionen erlauben würden, zu schaffen und individuell zu gestalten, das den Anforderungen des Besitzers entspricht. Fenster und Stauraumbereiche sind die senkrechten Hauptflächen, die zwischen Boden und Decke eingeflochten werden.

Pour l'appartement n°8, les indications du client étaient simples : créer une maison aussi grande que l'espace et ses fonctions le permettraient, personnalisée selon les exigences des propriétaires. Les fenêtres et les rangements constituent les principales surfaces verticales interposées entre le sol et le plafond.

En el caso de Flat 8, el deseo del cliente era sencillo: crear una casa tan grande como permitiese el espacio y sus funcionalidades, y que estuviese personalizada para atender sus requerimientos. Entre el suelo y el techo solo se interponen ventanas y espacios de almacenamiento, como principales superficies verticales.

www.designeightfivetwo.com // Team: Norman Ung

The apartment includes a living area and a bedroom. They can either be seamlessly connected to create an ample open space filled with light, or can be completely separated from one another to satisfy privacy needs. The flexible character of the apartments layout was a must to make the most of the limited space.

Die Wohnung umfasst einen Wohnbereich und ein Schlafzimmer. Sie können entweder nahtlos verbunden, wodurch ein großzügiger offener Raum entsteht, der mit Licht gefüllt ist, oder vollständig voneinander getrennt werden, wodurch der Bedarf an Privatsphäre gestillt wird. Der flexible Charakter des Wohnungsgrundrisses war ein Muss, um aus dem begrenzten Platz das Beste zu machen.

Cet appartement comprend une pièce à vivre et une chambre. Les deux pièces peuvent être reliées entre elles pour créer un grand espace ouvert lumineux ou être complètement séparées l'une de l'autre pour des besoins d'intimité. Un agencement flexible était une nécessité pour tirer le meilleur avantage de l'espace réduit.

El apartamento incluye un salón y un dormitorio. Se pueden unir para crear un espacio amplio y abierto lleno de luz o pueden estar completamente separados para satisfacer las necesidades de privacidad. El carácter flexible de la distribución de los apartamentos era un requisito indispensable para aprovechar al máximo el reducido espacio.

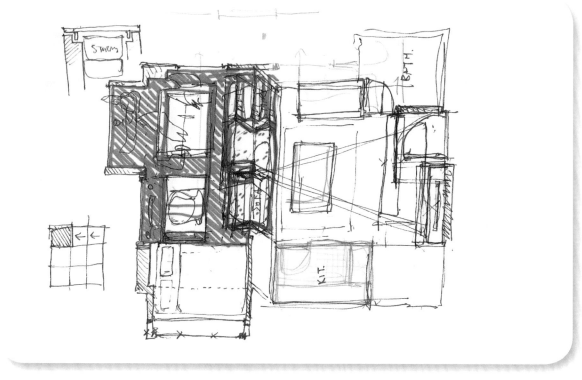

Conceptual design sketch

In the living area, a table that can extend in the occasion of family gatherings and various pullout drawers are the key elements of the design aimed at making efficient use of space.

Im Wohnbereich lässt sich ein Tisch bei Familienfeiern ausziehen, und verschiedene Schubfächer sind die Schlüsselelemente der Planung, die darauf abzielt, den Platz effizient zu nutzen.

Dans le séjour, on peut déployer une table à l'occasion de réunions de famille. Différents tiroirs constituent les éléments clés de cet agencement visant à utiliser efficacement l'espace disponible.

En el salón, una mesa que puede desplegarse para celebrar reuniones familiares y varios cajones son la clave del diseño, destinado a hacer un uso eficiente del espacio.

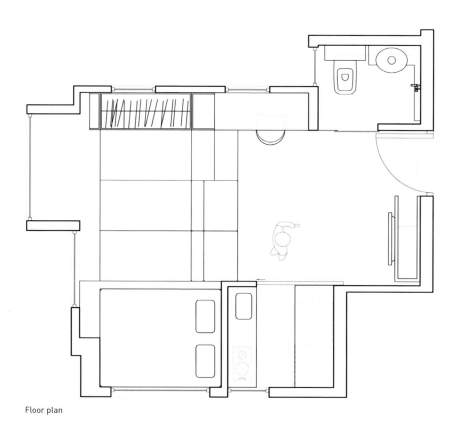

Floor plan

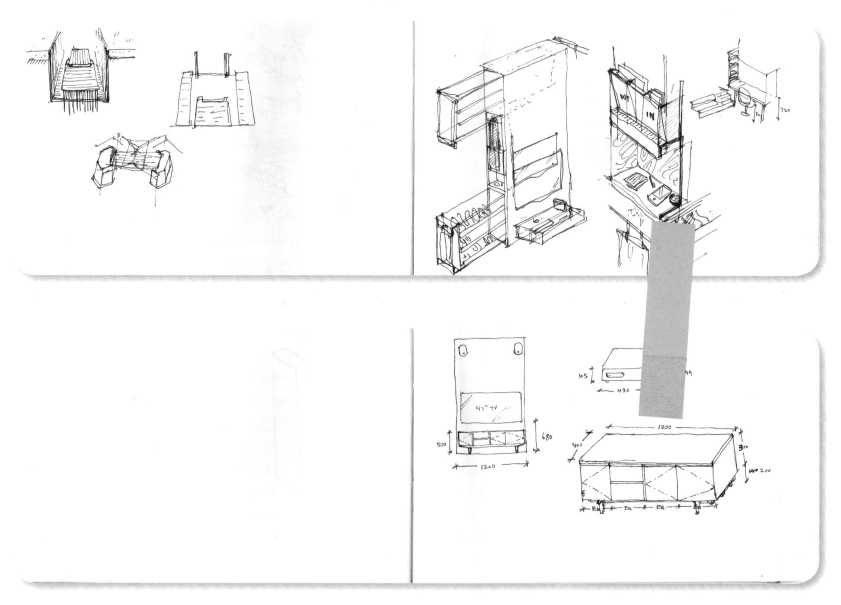

Conceptual design sketch

Movable partitions and oversized doors pair up with various creative storage solutions to provide the space with a clutter-free, comfortable atmosphere.

Bewegliche Trennwände und überdimensionierte Türen gesellen sich zu verschiedenen kreativen Stauraumlösungen, die dem Raum eine komfortable und aufgeräumte Atmosphäre verleihen.

Des cloisons mobiles et des portes surdimensionnées s'accordent avec différentes solutions créatives pour apporter une atmosphère désencombrée et confortable à l'espace.

Las particiones móviles y las puertas de gran tamaño se combinan con varias soluciones creativas de almacenamiento para dar lugar a un espacio al que rodea una atmósfera ordenada y cómoda.

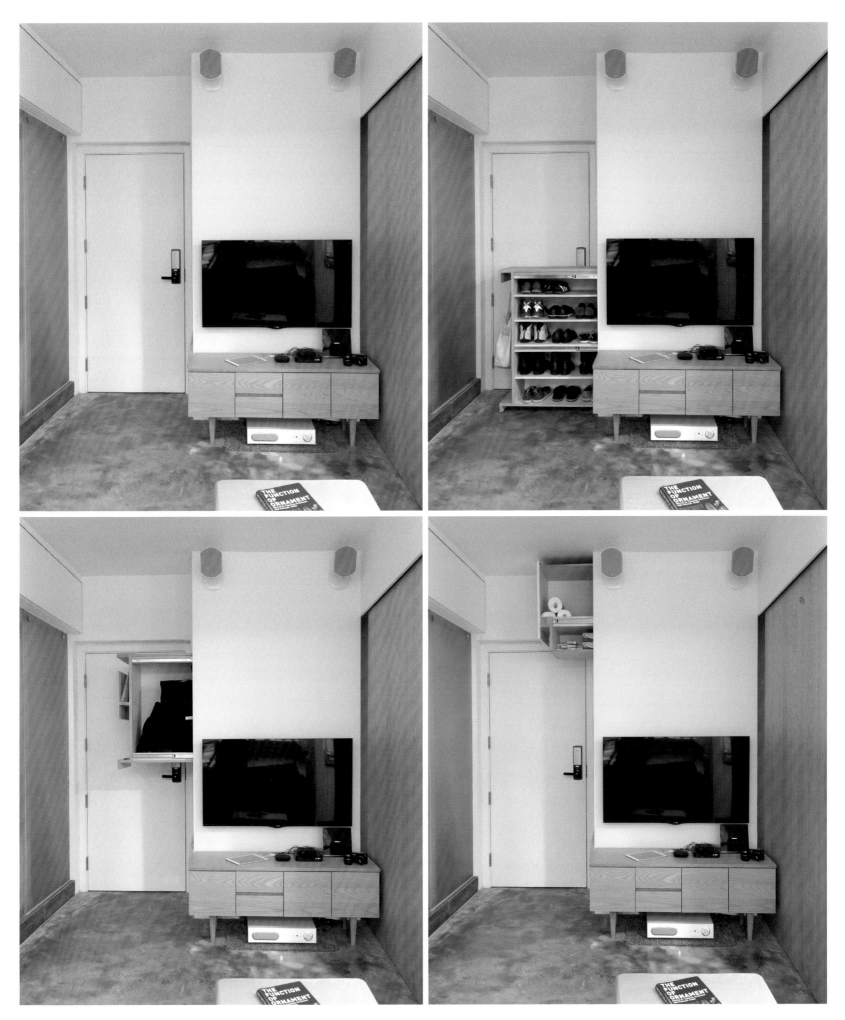

24 m² // 258 sq ft

Photo © Ruijing Photo

NANLUOGUXIANG HUTONG // B.L.U.E. ARCHITECTURE STUDIO
BEIJING, CHINA

Despite the small size of the site, the design offers comfortable living for a family of five. Yet, it presented an important challenge: the configuration of the new space had to balance family life and the need for privacy.

Trotz der geringen Größe der Wohnung bietet diese Planung einer fünfköpfigen Familie komfortables Wohnen. Dennoch stellte der Entwurf eine bedeutende Herausforderung dar: Die Gestaltung des neuen Raumes sollte Familienleben und das Bedürfnis nach Privatsphäre in Einklang bringen.

En dépit de l'étroitesse du lieu, son aménagement a permis de créer un espace de vie confortable pour une famille de cinq personnes. Cependant, un défi important a dû être relevé : configurer l'espace pour répondre à la fois aux besoins d'une vie familiale et aux besoins d'intimité de chacun des habitants.

A pesar de su pequeño tamaño, el diseño hace posible una vida cómoda para una familia de cinco. Aún así, presentaba un reto importante: la configuración del nuevo espacio debía equilibrar la vida familiar con la necesidad de privacidad.

www.b-l-u-e.net // Team: Shuhei Aoyama, Yoko Fujii, Yufeng Di, and Hanlin Yang

Design developmenmt sketches

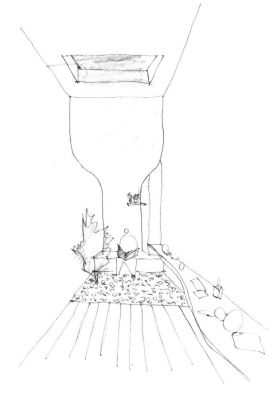

Multifunctional furnishings and innovative storage solutions were key to the creation of a space-efficient, yet comfortable living environment.

Multifunktionale Einrichtungsgegenstände und innovative Stauraumlösungen waren der Schlüssel zur Schaffung eines platzsparenden und dennoch komfortablen Wohnraums.

Un mobilier multifonctionnel et des solutions de rangement innovantes étaient essentiels pour créer un environnement de vie optimisant l'espace tout en restant confortable.

El mobiliario multifuncional y las innovadoras soluciones de almacenamiento fueron claves para la creación de un entorno eficiente y cómodo.

Building section

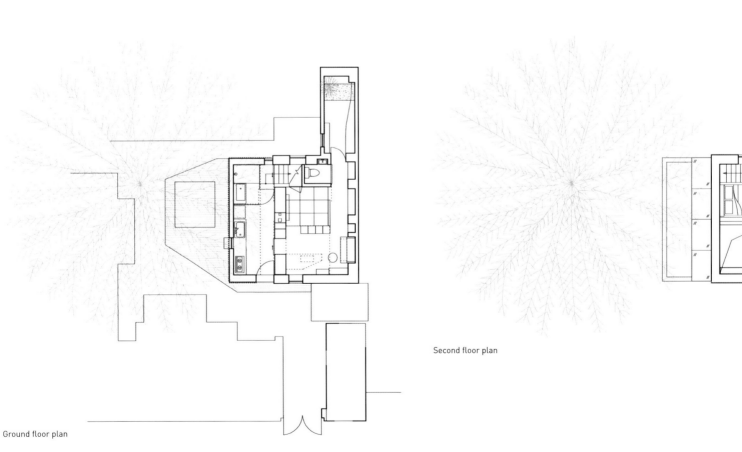

Ground floor plan

Second floor plan

The main goal was to incorporate as many storage solutions as possible, including the lining of walls with shelves and cabinets, and multifunctional spaces such as the dining and living room, which doubles as a bedroom.

Hauptziel war, so viele Stauraumlösungen wie möglich einzubinden, darunter das Auskleiden der Wände mit Regalen und Schränken, und Multifunktionsräume wie das Ess- und Wohnzimmer, das auch als Schlafzimmer dient.

L'objectif principal était d'incorporer autant de solutions de rangement que possible en doublant les murs avec des étagères et des placards et en créant des espaces multifonctionnels comme le salon-séjour qui peut se transformer en chambre.

El objetivo principal era incorporar tantas soluciones de almacenamiento como fuera posible, incluyendo el revestimiento de paredes con estantes y armarios además de espacios multifuncionales como el comedor y salón, que también funciona como dormitorio.

Shelves at seat height line the walls whenever possible to promote interaction among family members.

Regale auf Sitzhöhe säumen die Wände, wann immer möglich, um die Interaktion zwischen den Familienmitgliedern zu fördern.

Les étagères à hauteur d'assise suivent les murs lorsque cela est possible pour favoriser l'interaction entre membres de la famille.

Donde es posible, hay estantes en las paredes que funcionan como asientos, para promover la interacción entre los miembros de la familia.

43 m² // 463 sq ft

Photo © Ruijing Photo

DENGSHIKOU HUTONG RESIDENCE // B.L.U.E. ARCHITECTURE STUDIO
BEIJING, CHINA

An L-shaped site accommodates a home for a family of six, squeezed between a masonry wall facing the street and a two-story building. The design is a *tour de force* displaying outstanding space-saving solutions that promote multifunctionality without sacrificing comfort in a space of limited dimensions.

Ein L-förmiger Bereich beherbergt das Zuhause einer sechsköpfigen Familie, das sich zur Straße hin zwischen eine Mauerwand und ein zweigeschossiges Gebäude schmiegt. Der Entwurf ist eine *Tour de force* und präsentiert hervorragende Platzsparlösungen, die der Multifunktionalität zugutekommen, ohne in einem Raum mit begrenzten Dimensionen auf Komfort zu verzichten.

Une famille de six est logée dans cette habitation en forme de L glissée entre un mur maçonné face à la rue et un immeuble de deux étages. C'est un véritable tour de force des architectes qui ont su trouver des solutions pour économiser l'espace et la rendre fonctionnelle sans sacrifier le confort dans ce lieu aux dimensions limitées.

El solar en forma de L acomoda una casa para una familia de seis, encajado entre una pared de mampostería que da a la calle y un edificio de dos pisos. El diseño es un *tour de force* que muestra sobresalientes soluciones de ahorro de espacio que promueven la multifuncionalidad sin sacrificar el confort dentro de un espacio de dimensiones limitadas.

www.b-l-u-e.net // Team: Shuhei Aoyama, Yoko Fujii, and Lingzi Liu

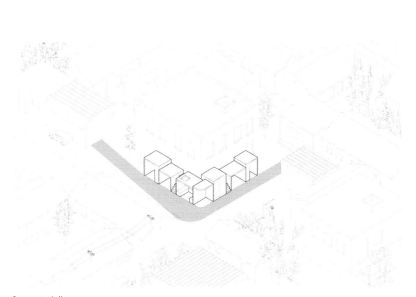

Conceptual diagram

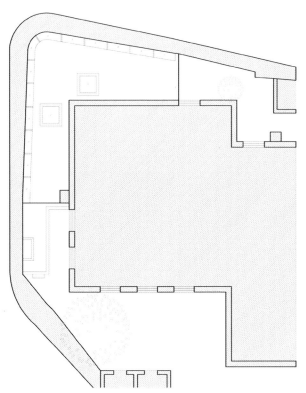

Roof plan

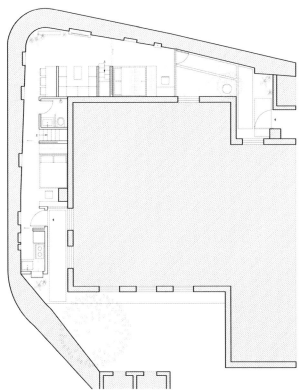

Ground floor plan

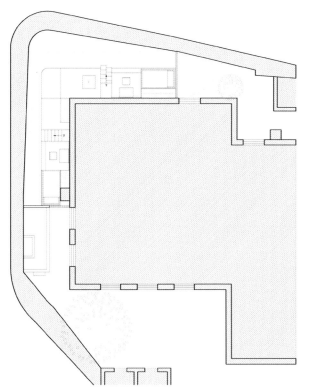

Second floor plan

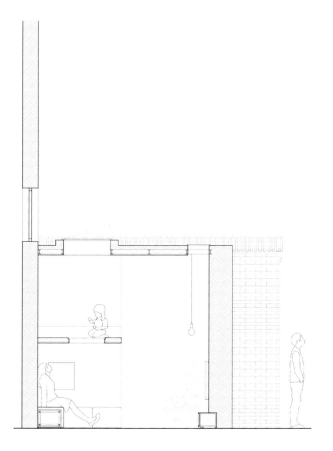

Building sections

The house contains seven wooden boxes, each dedicated to a specific function. The functional program of these boxes determined their size and proportion.

Das Haus umfasst sieben Holzkästen, von denen jeder eine eigene Funktion hat. Die funktionelle Anwendung dieser Kästen bestimmte deren Größe und Proportionen.

Cette maison contient sept unités, chacune vouée à une fonction spécifique. L'usage prévu pour celles-ci a déterminé leur taille et leurs proportions.

La casa contiene siete cajas de madera, cada una con una función específica. La funcionalidad de estas cajas determinó su tamaño y proporción.

Through a cleverly though-through track system, the boxes can expand or shrink, revealing extra storage or foldaway tables at any given time.

Durch ein klug durchdachtes Schienensystem lassen sich die Kästen vergrößern oder verkleinern und dabei jederzeit zusätzlichen Stauraum oder Klapptische zum Vorschein bringen.

Par le biais d'un système de rails bien pensé, ces caissons peuvent être agrandis ou réduits pour procurer du rangement supplémentaire ou des tables pliantes à tout moment.

A través de un ingenioso sistema de raíles muy bien pensado, las cajas pueden expandirse o contraerse, dejando ver más almacenamiento o mesas plegables en cualquier momento.

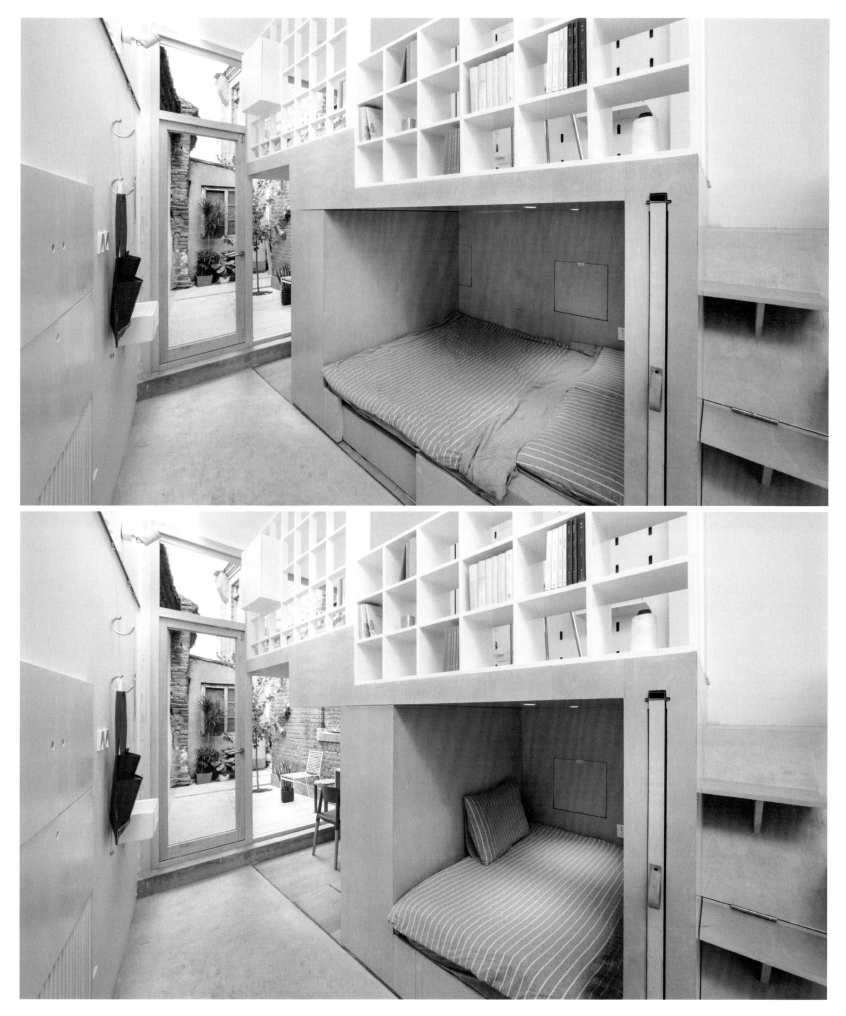

The leftover space generates a continuous open space that promotes interaction between family members, while a series of sliding panels ensure that each family member can enjoy their own private space.

Der restliche Raum schafft einen durchgehenden offenen Raum, der die Interaktion unter den Familienmitgliedern fördert, während eine Reihe von Schiebepaneelen sicherstellt, dass jedes Familienmitglied seinen eigenen Privatbereich genießen kann.

La surface restante est un espace ouvert continu qui permet les interactions entre les membres de la famille, tandis qu'une série de panneaux coulissants assure à chacun d'eux un espace privé.

El espacio sobrante genera un espacio continuo abierto que promueve la interacción entre los miembros de la familia, mientras que una serie de paneles deslizantes garantizan su privacidad.

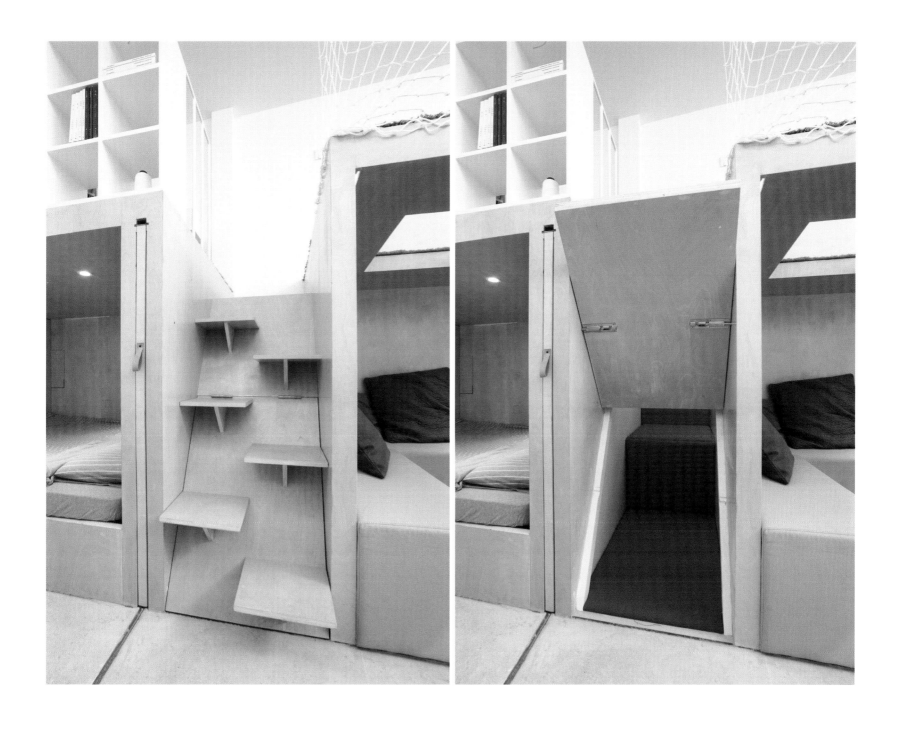

An open space on the second floor accommodates a sleeping area for the youngest of the family, a playroom and a library.

Ein offener Raum im zweiten Stock beherbergt einen Schlafbereich für die Jüngsten der Familie, ein Spielzimmer und eine Bibliothek.

Un espace ouvert au premier étage accueille un coin sieste pour le cadet de la famille, une salle de jeu et une bibliothèque.

El espacio abierto del primer piso tiene una zona de descanso para el benjamín de la familia, una sala de juegos y una biblioteca.

The project offered unlimited design opportunities to explore ways or the optimization of the space available in order to fulfil the functional requirements and satisfy the need for abundant storage.

Das Projekt bot unbegrenzte Gestaltungsmöglichkeiten, um die Optimierung des Raumes zu erforschen, um die Anforderungen an die Funktion zu erfüllen und dem Bedarf an großzügigen Mengen an Stauraum gerecht zu werden.

Ce projet a offert l'opportunité aux architectes d'explorer différentes solutions pour optimiser un espace réduit tout en répondant à des exigences de fonctionnalité et à la nécessité d'avoir de nombreux rangements.

El proyecto ofreció un diseño con infinitas posibilidades para explorar formas u optimizar el espacio disponible, con el fin de cumplir con los requisitos funcionales y satisfacer la necesidad de gran almacenamiento existente.

Natural light, brought into the home through various skylights, is a critical element of the design, contributing to the creation of an interior space that feels larger that it actually is.

Natürliches Licht, das durch verschiedene Oberlichter in das Heim fällt, ist ein wichtiges Gestaltungselement des Entwurfs und trägt zur Schaffung eines Innenraumes bei, der größer wirkt, als er tatsächlich ist.

La lumière naturelle, guidée vers l'intérieur par différents puits de jour, est un élément crucial contribuant à créer un espace intérieur qui a l'air plus grand qu'il ne l'est en réalité.

Un elemento crucial del diseño es la luz natural, llevada a la casa a través de varias claraboyas, que contribuyen a la creación de un espacio interior que parece más grande de lo que realmente es.

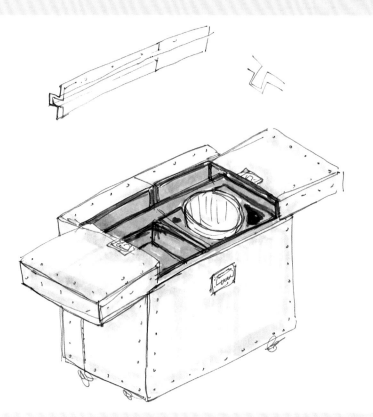

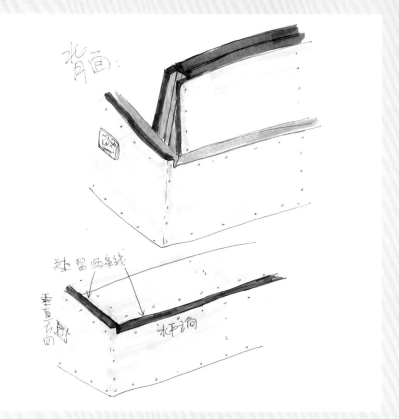

BUILDING WARDROBE // NAIHAN LI

www.naihanli.com

The wardrobe is shaped like the CCTV Tower in Beijing, designed by the Dutch architecture firm OMA. Complete with the exact pattern that wraps the building's facades, it is part of a line of furniture that features miniaturizations of emblematic buildings, including a bookcase shaped like The Pentagon.

Von der Form her ähnelt dieser Schrank dem CCTV Tower in Peking, entworfen wurde er von dem holländischen Architekturbüro OMA. Samt dem genauen Muster, das die Fassaden des Gebäudes umfasst, ist er Teil einer Möbelserie, die Verkleinerungen von Kultgebäude vorstellt, darunter ein Bücherregal in der Form des Pentagons.

Cette armoire a la forme de la CCTV Tower de Beijing, conçue par le cabinet d'architecture hollandais OMA. Ornée des mêmes motifs que ceux qui entourent les façades de ce bâtiment, elle fait partie d'une ligne de meubles qui reproduisent en miniature des immeubles emblématiques (il existe notamment une bibliothèque en forme du Pentagone.

El armario tiene la forma de la Torre CCTV de Pekín y ha sido diseñado por la firma holandesa de arquitectura OMA. Terminado con el mismo patrón que envuelve las fachadas de los edificios, es parte de una línea de muebles que se caracteriza por miniaturizar edificios emblemáticos, como por ejemplo una librería con forma del Pentágono.

Prototype
Material: Brazilian rosewood

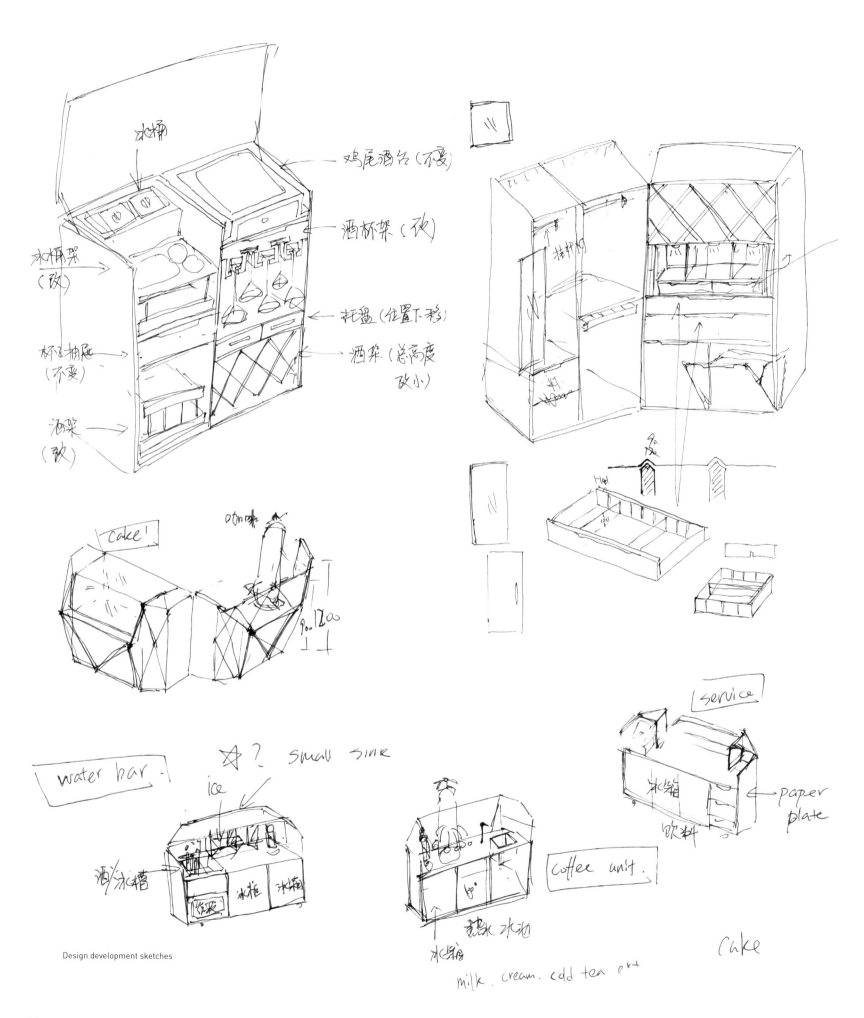

水桶

鸡尾酒台（不变）

酒杯架（改）

水桶架（改）

托盘（位置下移）

杯子抽屉（不变）

酒架（总高度改小）

酒架（改）

排杯架

cake!

Coffee

service

water bar.

☆? small sink

ice

paper plate

酒/水槽

coffee unit.

热水物

水桶

Cake

milk. cream. cold tea ort

Design development sketches

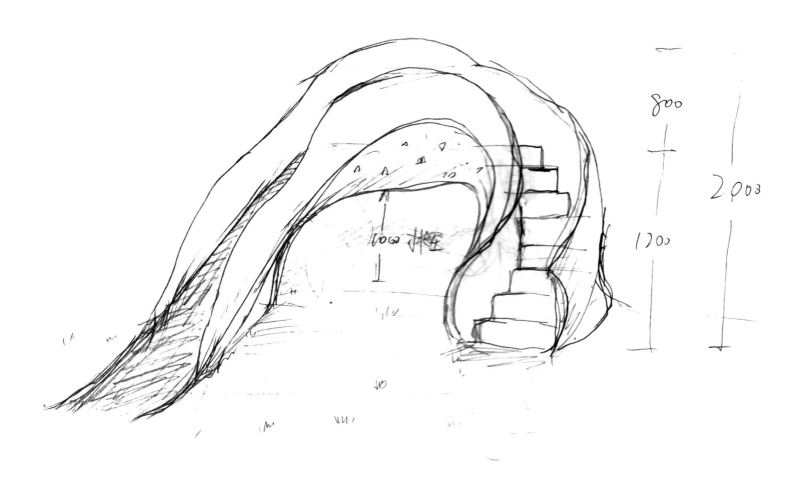

800

2000

1000

1000

1300

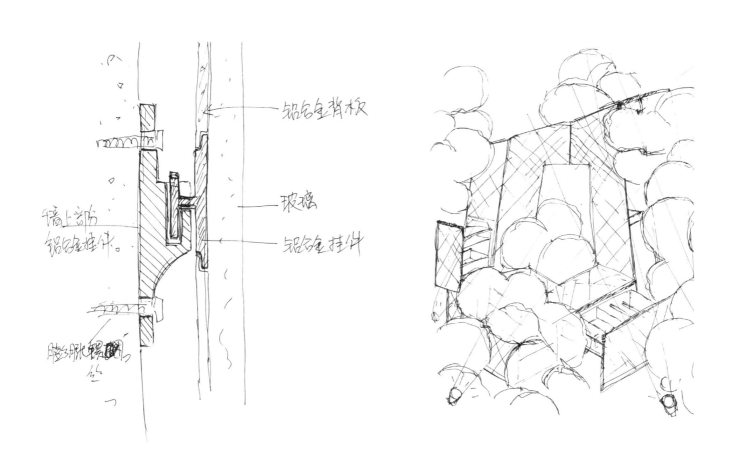

铝合金背板

玻璃

铝合金挂件

墙上部分
铝合金挂件。

膨胀螺栓

86 m² // 926 sq ft

Photo © Antonio Duarte, C. Baechtold, V. Vincenzo

QUATRE SEPTEMBRE APARTMENT // ALIA BENGANA
PARIS, FRANCE

When the client, a photojournalist, bought the apartment, it was unfit for habitation. He wanted a modern space with a guestroom and a multi purpose living area that could accommodate a dining area, a kitchen, and an office.

Als der Kunde, ein Fotoreporter, die Wohnung kaufte, eignete sie sich nicht als Behausung. Er wünschte sich einen modernen Raum mit einem Gästezimmer und einem Mehrzweckwohnbereich, der Essbereich, Küche und ein Büro unterbringen konnte.

Lorsque le client, un photojournaliste, a acheté cet appartement, ce dernier n'était pas habitable. Il voulait un espace moderne comprenant une chambre d'amis et une pièce à vivre polyvalente qui puisse accueillir un coin-repas, une cuisine et un bureau.

Cuando el cliente, reportero gráfico, compró este apartamento, no era habitable. Quería una vivienda moderna, con habitación de invitados y una zona de estar multiusos en la que pudiera albergar una zona de comedor, una cocina y una oficina.

www.aliabengana.com // Team: Alia Bengana and Thomas Buckenmeyer

This living area can fulfil the functions of a kitchen and dining room thanks to a system of retractable furniture.

Dank eines Systems von versenkbaren Möbeln kann dieser Wohnbereich die Funktionen einer Küche und eines Esszimmers erfüllen.

La pièce à vivre peut remplir les fonctions d'une cuisine et d'un coin-repas grâce à un système de mobilier escamotable.

El sistema de muebles retráctiles permite que la zona de estar sea también cocina y comedor.

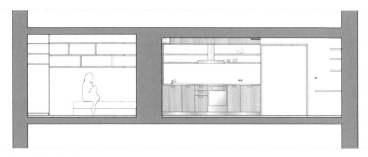

Longitudinal section

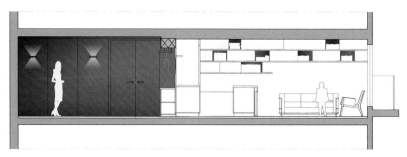

Cross section

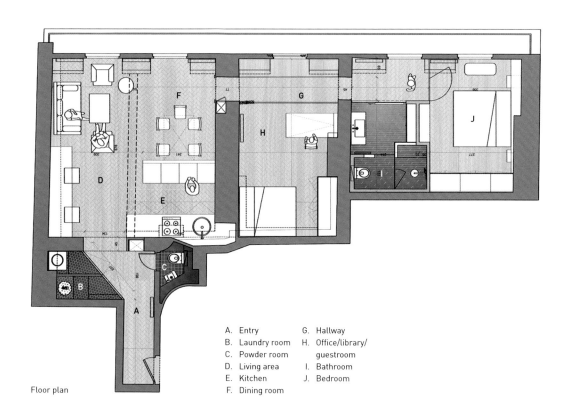

Floor plan

A. Entry
B. Laundry room
C. Powder room
D. Living area
E. Kitchen
F. Dining room
G. Hallway
H. Office/library/
guestroom
I. Bathroom
J. Bedroom

The design emphasizes the contrast between the dark entry hall and the bright living area. A funnel effect is achieved by building a closet diagonally in the hallway. It conceals the laundry room and the utility closet.

Der Entwurf unterstreicht den Kontrast zwischen der dunklen Eingangshalle und dem hellen Wohnbereich. Ein Trichtereffekt wird erzielt, indem man im Flur diagonal eine kleine Kammer errichtet, darin verbergen sich die Waschküche und ein Putzmittelschrank.

Cet aménagement souligne le contraste entre l'aspect sombre du hall d'entrée et la clarté de la pièce à vivre. Un effet d'entonnoir est provoqué par la construction d'un placard en diagonale dans le couloir. Celui-ci cache la buanderie et le placard à balais.

El diseño enfatiza el contraste entre la oscura zona de entrada y la sala de estar, llena de luz. El efecto embudo se consigue gracias a la incorporación de un armario diagonal en el pasillo, que oculta la zona de servicio y un armario.

In the guest bedroom, which doubles as a library, a desk folds away against the wall when not needed to free up some space. Along the window wall, a storage bench facilitates the access to the balcony.

Im Gästeschlafzimmer, das auch als Bibliothek dient, lässt sich ein Schreibtisch gegen die Wand klappen, wenn er nicht benötigt wird, um etwas Platz zu schaffen. Entlang der Fensterwand ermöglicht eine Bank mit Stauraum den Zugang zum Balkon.

Dans la chambre d'amis, qui sert également de bibliothèque, un bureau est plié contre le mur lorsqu'il n'est pas utilisé pour libérer de l'espace. Le long du mur côté fenêtre, une banquette de rangement facilite l'accès au balcon.

En la habitación de invitados, que también puede usarse como biblioteca, una mesa se pliega en la pared cuando no se usa, para liberar el espacio. A lo largo de la pared de la ventana, un banco de almacenaje permite el acceso al balcón.

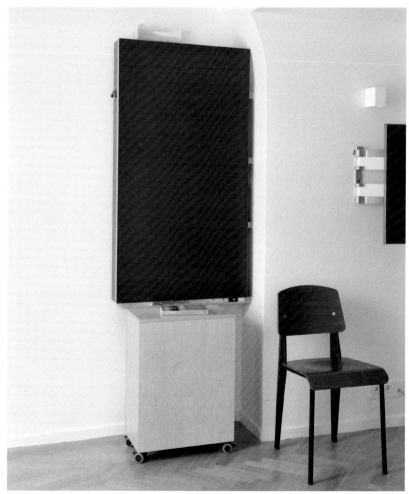

37 m² // 398 sq ft

Photo © Patryk Lewinski

BRANDBURG HOME AND STUDIO // MODE:LINA

POZNAŃ, POLAND

The brief for the redesign of a space called for a comfortable living place and an attractive work environment. The challenge the architect faced was to incorporate all the functions into a limited area. Further, the entire place had to be safe for a six-year old boy, who would also have his own "hiding place".

Die Vorgabe für die Neugestaltung dieses Raumes verlangte einen bequemen Wohnraum und ein attraktives Arbeitsumfeld. Die Herausforderung, mit der der Architekt konfrontiert war, lautete, alle Funktionen in einen begrenzten Bereich zu integrieren. Außerdem musste der gesamte Ort für einen sechsjährigen Jungen sicher sein, der auch sein eigenes „Versteck" haben sollte.

L'énoncé de projet de réaménagement de l'espace citait un lieu de vie confortable et un environnement de travail attrayant. Le défi de l'architecte a été de réussir à intégrer toutes les fonctions dans un espace limité. En outre, tout endroit devait être sans danger pour un petit garçon de six ans qui devait également avoir sa propre « cachette ».

El objetivo de la reestructuración del espacio era convertirlo en un hogar cómodo y un lugar atractivo de trabajo. El reto para el arquitecto fue incorporar todas las funcionalidades en un espacio limitado. Además, debía ser un lugar seguro para um niño de seis años, quien también tendría su propio «escondite».

www.modelina-architekci.com // Team: Pawel Garus, Jerzy Wozniak, and Kinga Kin

The architect designed a plywood box that integrates a kitchen, an office, a loft bed, and a cleverly concealed "hiding room" for the young boy. There is also a "secret" base that works as toy box just behind a movable shelf unit.

Der Architekt entwarf einen Furnierholz-kasten, der eine Küche, einen Büroraum, ein Loft-Bett und ein geschickt verborge-nes Versteck für den kleinen Jungen in-tegrierte. Es gibt auch einen „geheimen" Sockel, der direkt hinter einer beweglichen Regaleinheit als Spielzeugkasten fungiert.

L'architecte a conçu une enveloppe en contreplaqué intégrant une cuisine, un bu-reau, un lit mezzanine et une « cachette » habilement dissimulée pour le petit garçon. Il y a aussi la base « secrète » qui sert de coffre à jouets juste derrière l'unité de ran-gement mobile.

El arquitecto diseñó una caja de madera contrachapada que integraba cocina, ofi-cina, cama alta y un ingenioso "escondite" para el niño. También hay un espacio "se-creto" que funciona como caja de juguetes justo detrás de la estantería móvil.

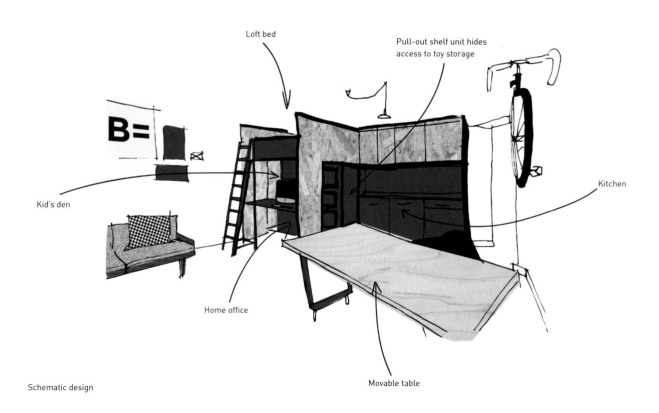

Loft bed

Pull-out shelf unit hides
access to toy storage

Kid's den

Kitchen

Home office

Movable table

Schematic design

Numerous shelves, drawers, and cabinets are carefully integrated into the design of the black wood box, freeing-up floor space, hence creating a comfortable and roomy live and work environment.

Zahlreiche Regale, Schubladen und Schränke sind sorgfältig in die Formgebung des schwarzen Holzkastens integriert und machen Nutzfläche frei, wodurch eine komfortable und geräumige Wohn- und Arbeitsumgebung geschaffen wird.

Plusieurs étagères, tiroirs, et placards sont soigneusement intégrés dans le design du module en bois noir, ce qui libère de l'espace au sol, créant ainsi un environnement de vie et de travail confortable et spacieux.

Se integraron muchas estanterías, cajones y armarios en el diseño de la caja de madera oscura, liberando el espacio y consiguiendo así un entorno de trabajo y ocio confortable y espacioso.

220 m² // 2,368 sq ft

Photo © Jonathan Maloney

ART COLLECTOR'S LOFT // MASS OPERATIONS

HONG KONG, SAR CHINA

The owner of this loft is an art collector, and as such, his wish was to be able to display his art and book collections in an open space suitable for entertaining. The layout of the loft uses a concrete wall to separate the public and private areas and serves as support for artwork.

Der Besitzer des Lofts ist Kunstsammler und als solcher lautete sein Wunsch, imstande zu sein, seine Kunst- und Büchersammlungen in einem offenen Raum ausstellen zu können, der auch für die Bewirtung von Gästen geeignet ist. Der Grundriss des Lofts nutzt eine Betonwand als Abtrennung von Gemeinschafts- und Privatbereichen und dient als Unterlage für die Kunstwerke.

Le propriétaire du loft est un collectionneur qui souhaitait pouvoir présenter ses collections d'œuvres d'art et de livres dans un espace ouvert et adapté pour recevoir des invités. Un mur en béton sépare les espaces publics et privés et permet d'accrocher les œuvres d'art.

El propietario de este *loft* es un coleccionista de arte que deseaba un espacio donde poder recibir invitados y a la vez mostrar su colección de libros y de arte. El diseño del *loft* utiliza un muro de hormigón que separa las estancias públicas y privadas además de servir como soporte a las obras de arte expuestas.

www.massoperations.com // Team: Viviano Villarreal-Buerón

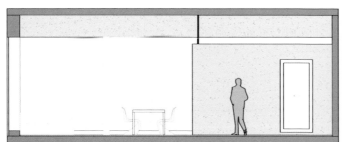

Section A

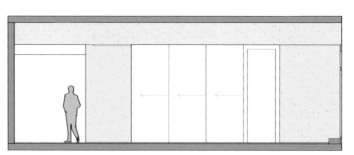

Section B

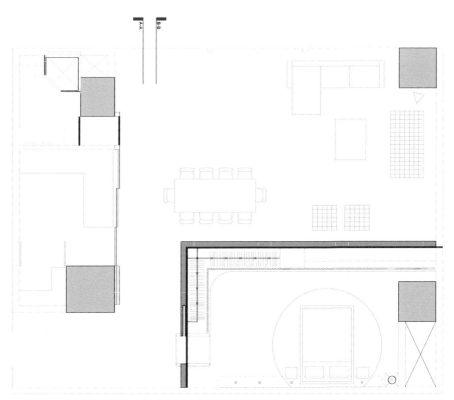

Floor plan

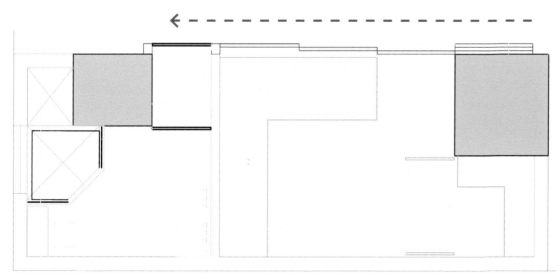

Sliding blackboard panels at kitchen

Opening and closing devices are used to conceal and reveal areas. The kitchen can be hidden or exposed by means of large sliding panels that double as blackboards, creating a dynamic public area.

Vorrichtungen zum Öffnen und Schließen werden dazu verwendet, Bereiche zu verbergen und freizulegen. Die Küche kann mithilfe großer Schiebepaneele, die zusammengefaltet werden und einen dynamischen Gemeinschaftsbereich schaffen, verborgen oder exponiert werden.

Des dispositifs d'ouverture et de fermeture permettent de révéler ou de dissimuler les espaces. La cuisine peut être cachée ou visible grâce à de grands panneaux coulissants qui servent aussi de tableaux noirs, créant ainsi un espace de vie dynamique.

Para ocultar y mostrar estancias, se usan elementos de apertura y cierre. La cocina se esconde o se muestra por medio de grandes paneles/pizarras deslizantes, que aportan dinamismo a esta zona.

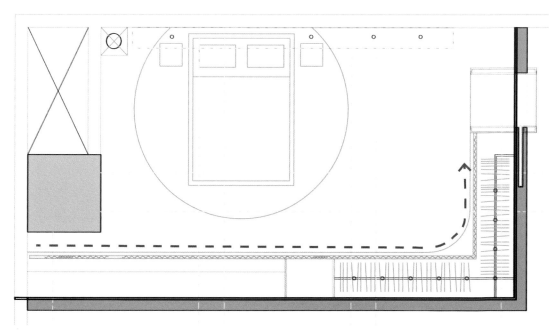

Room divider curtain

The bedroom has a curtain to hide the wardrobe whenever is not needed. The curtain changes the character of the space, transforming the bedroom into a dressing room with a swift pull of the curtain.

Das Schlafzimmer hat einen Vorhang, der den Schrank verbirgt, solange dieser nicht erforderlich ist. Der Vorhang verändert den Charakter des Raumes und verwandelt das Schlafzimmer durch schnelles Vorziehen des Vorhangs in ein Umkleidezimmer.

Dans la chambre, un rideau dissimule le dressing lorsqu'il n'est pas utilisé. Ce rideau transforme l'espace qui passe d'une chambre à un dressing et ce, en un simple coup de rideau.

El dormitorio tiene una cortina que esconde el armario cuando no se usa. La cortina cambia el carácter del espacio, transformando el dormitorio en un vestidor simplemente con un ligero movimiento de la misma.

200 m² // 2,152 sq ft

Photo © penda

ART STORAGE // PENDA

HONG KONG, SAR CHINA

This project consisted in the design of a home, not for people, but for artwork. A copper suitcase-like box can be fully unfolded and integrated in the space for the display of art, and folded up to store the artwork securely. The box may not be for human living, but does contain a couch, a bar, and a working desk in addition to a sliding drawer for artwork.

Bei diesem Projekt ging es um die Gestaltung eines Zuhauses, doch dieses Mal nicht für Menschen, sondern für Kunstwerke. Ein kofferähnlicher Kupferkasten kann ganz aufgeklappt und für die Darstellung von Kunst in den Raum integriert und zusammengeklappt werden, um die Kunstwerke sicher zu verwahren. Der Kasten mag nicht für menschliches Leben gedacht sein, enthält jedoch neben einer Schublade für Kunstwerke eine Couch, eine Bar und einen Schreibtisch.

Pour ce projet, il s'agissait de concevoir une maison non pas pour des personnes, mais pour des œuvres d'art. Un module en cuivre ressemblant à une valise peut être totalement déplié et intégré dans l'espace pour exposer des œuvres, et replié pour les stocker en toute sécurité. Ce module a beau ne pas être destiné à un usage quotidien, il contient néanmoins un sofa, un bar et un bureau en plus d'un tiroir coulissant destiné à accueillir des créations artistiques.

Este proyecto consistió en el diseño de una vivienda no para ser habitada, sino para ser una obra de arte. Una caja de cobre en forma de maletín puede ser desplegada e integrada en el espacio para mostrar las obras de arte y plegada para almacenarlas con seguridad. La caja puede no ser habitable, pero contiene un sofá, un bar y un escritorio de trabajo además de un cajón deslizante para las obras de arte.

www.home-of-penda.com // Team: Chris Precht, Sun Dayong, Bai Xue, Quan He, and Li Pengchong

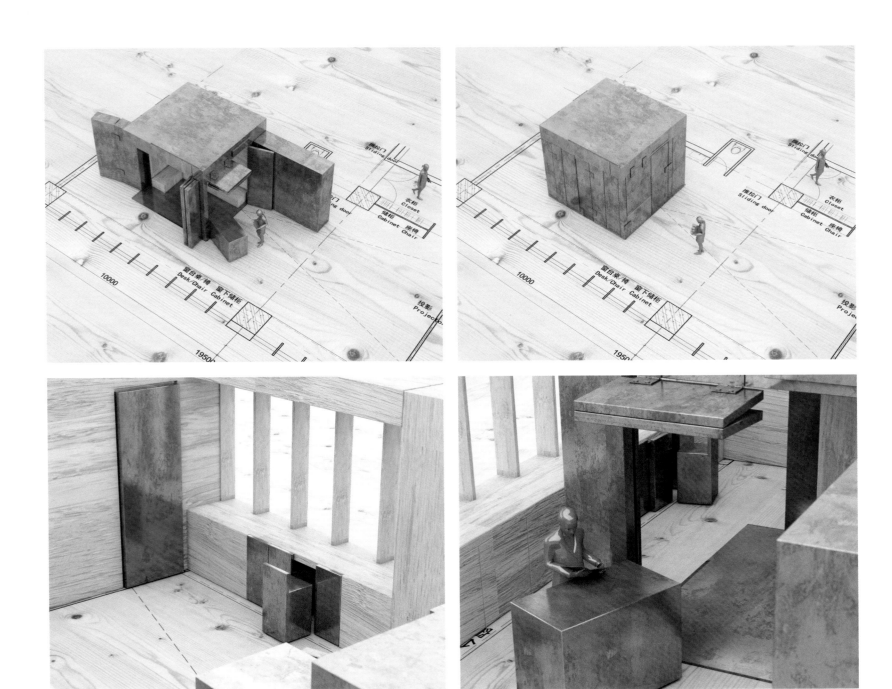

Views of scale model

FROM A BOX TO AN INTEGRATING OBJECT

Conceptual diagram

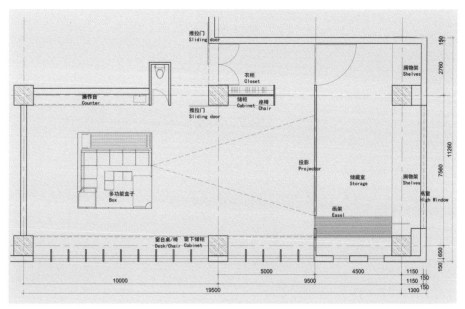

Floor plan A

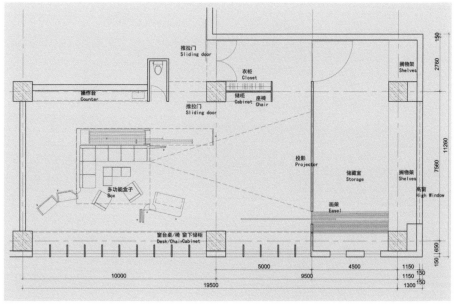

Floor plan B

The all-concrete apartment is to the copper box what the latter is to the artwork it contains: a container within a container.

Diese Wohnung ganz aus Beton ist für den Kupferkasten das, was letzterer für die Kunstwerke ist, die er enthält: Ein Behälter innerhalb eines Behälters.

L'appartement bétonné est au module en cuivre ce que celui-ci est aux œuvres d'art qu'il contient : un contenant dans un contenant.

El apartamento de hormigón es a la caja de cobre lo que esta es a las obras de arte: un contenedor dentro de un contenedor.

Additional storage and seating is provided along the long wall with windows. The design of these elements is in line with that of the copper box.

Zusätzlicher Stauraum und zusätzliche Sitzplätze werden an der Längswand mit Fenstern bereitgestellt. Die Gestaltung dieser Elemente steht in Einklang mit der des Kupferkastens.

Rangement et assise supplémentaires suivent le long mur percé de fenêtres. Le design de ces éléments est dans la continuité de celui du module en cuivre.

A lo largo de la extensa pared con ventanas, se habilita espacio adicional para almacenaje y descanso. El diseño de estos elementos está en línea con el de la caja de cobre.

Photo © Akihiro Yoshida

NEST SHELF // NENDO

www.nendo.jp

This sliding shelving unit is made of carbon fibre panels, a material that is increasingly used in furniture manufacturing for its strength relative to its lightweight. The shelf can double its width. By doing so, not only can it increase its capacity for storage, but also the user can adjust its width to fit it in the space available.

Dieses Schieberegal besteht aus Carbonfaserverkleidungen, einem Material, das aufgrund seiner Stärke im Verhältnis zu seinem geringen Gewicht in zunehmendem Maße in der Möbelherstellung eingesetzt wird. Das Regal kann seine Breite verdoppeln. Dadurch kann es nicht nur seine Stauraumkapazität erhöhen, sondern der Benutzer kann auch seine Breite einstellen und somit an den vorhandenen Raum anpassen.

Ce bloc d'étagères coulissantes est constitué de panneaux en fibre de carbone, un matériau qui est de plus en plus utilisé dans la fabrication de mobilier, autant pour sa résistance que pour sa légèreté. L'étagère peut être deux fois plus large. Dans ce cas, elle peut non seulement augmenter sa capacité de stockage, mais l'usager peut également ajuster sa largeur en fonction l'espace disponible.

Esta estantería deslizante está realizada en paneles de fibra de carbón, un material que se utiliza cada vez más en la fabricación de muebles por su firmeza en relación a su ligereza. El estante puede doblar su anchura. Al hacerlo, no solo aumenta su capacidad de almacenamiento, sino que permite al usuario poder regular el ancho para que se ajuste al espacio disponible.

Supported by TOKYO R&D COMPOSITE and Factori Hinoki
Materials: Carbon fiber panels, synthetic aramid fibre panels, and larch veneer

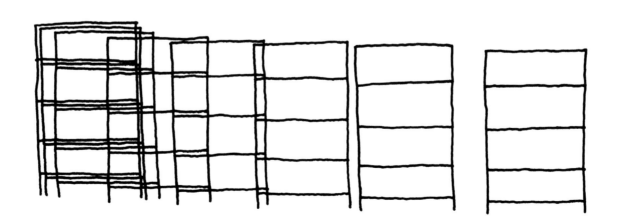

154 m² // 1,658 sq ft

Photo © Peter Bennetts Studio

TOY MANAGEMENT HOUSE // AUSTIN MAYNARD ARCHITECTS
MELBOURNE, VICTORIA, AUSTRALIA

The design for a house extension accommodates the needs of a female executive and her newborn child. The design of the extension's ground floor addresses the need for storage, and the maximization of floor area. The result is a raised floor that conceals a giant storage space and toy box.

Der Entwurf für eine Hauserweiterung erfüllt die Anforderungen einer weiblichen Führungskraft und deren neugeborener Kinder. Die Gestaltung der Erdgeschosserweiterung geht den Bedarf an Stauraum und die Maximierung der Nutzfläche an. Das Ergebnis ist ein Zwischenboden, der einen riesigen Stauraum und Spielzeugkasten verbirgt.

La conception d'une extension pour la maison répond aux besoins d'un cadre supérieur et de son nouveau-né. Le rez-de-chaussée a été conçu pour optimiser la surface en tenant compte de la nécessité de nombreux rangements : le sol, surélevé, dissimule d'immenses espaces de stockage et des coffres à jouets.

El diseño de esta ampliación resuelve las necesidades de una mujer ejecutiva y de su bebé recién nacido. En la planta baja se centra en la necesidad de almacenamiento y la maximización de la zona del suelo. El resultado es un suelo elevado que oculta un gran espacio de almacenamiento y una caja de juguetes.

www.maynardarchitects.com // Team: Andrew Maynard, Mark Austin, and Nathalie Miles

Generally, the downside of lining walls with cabinets is that the usable area is reduced. What if our storage space was within our floor? That was the question around which the architects developed a strikingly creative solution.

Im Allgemeinen haben Futterwände mit Schränken den Nachteil, dass die nutzbare Fläche verringert wird. Wie wäre es, wenn sich der Speicherplatz im Fußboden befände? Dies war die Frage, auf die die Architekten eine auffallend kreative Antwort parat hatten.

De manière générale, l'encastrement d'espaces de rangement dans les murs a l'inconvénient de réduire la surface utile. Et pourquoi ne pas agencer cet espace à l'étage ? Telle est la question sur laquelle se sont penchés les architectes pour développer un système singulièrement créatif.

En general, el inconveniente de las paredes revestidas con armarios es que el área utilizable se reduce. ¿Qué ocurre si nuestro espacio de almacenaje estuviera en el suelo? Esa fue la cuestión en torno a la cual los arquitectos desarrollaron una solución sorprendentemente creativa.

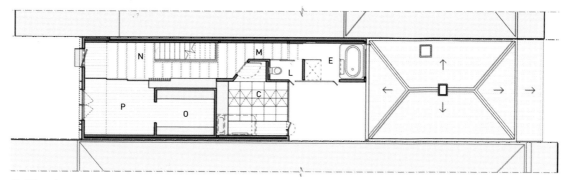

First floor plan

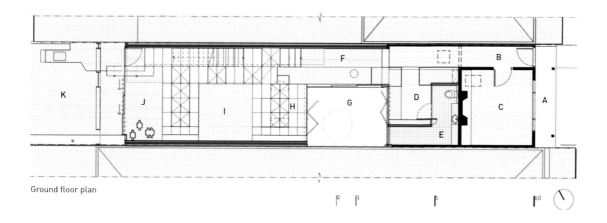

Ground floor plan

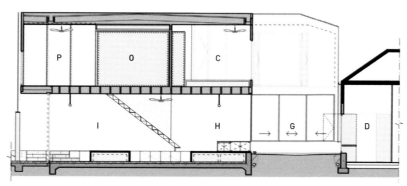

Longitudinal section

A. Porch
B. Entry hall
C. Bedroom
D. Study
E. Bathroom
F. Kitchen
G. Courtyard
H. Dining area
I. Lounge
J. Lounge pit
K. Backyard
L. Toilet room
M. Corridor
N. Landing
O. Walk-in closet
P. Master bedroom

Conceptual diagrams

The kitchen countertop is at seat height —roughly 45 centimetres— above the new floor. The architects designed an upholstered seat under a flap on the kitchen countertop, so that there can be an extra seat at the dining table.

Die Küchenarbeitsfläche befindet sich auf Sitzhöhe - etwa 45 Zentimeter - über dem neuen Boden. Unter einer Klappe an der Küchenarbeitsfläche entwarfen die Architekten einen gepolsterten Sitz, um einen zusätzlichen Platz am Esstisch zu schaffen.

Le plan de travail de la cuisine est à environ 45 centimètres au-dessus du nouveau sol. Les architectes ont conçu une assise matelassée sous une trappe sur le comptoir pour qu'il y ait un siège supplémentaire à table.

La encimera de la cocina está a la altura de un asiento, 45 centímetros aproximadamente, por encima del nuevo suelo. Los arquitectos diseñaron un asiento tapizado bajo una parte de la encimera de la cocina, pudiendo haber un asiento extra en la mesa de comedor.

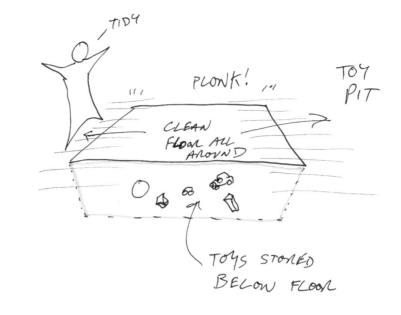

Beyond the need for storage, the architects were also concerned with the radical day-to-day changes a baby brings. We have all observed babies throw anything they can get a hold of to the floor and grown-ups pick them up. The architects actually turn this natural habit into the parents' ally, enabling the floor to "swallow" all the mess with a few swoops of a broom.

Über den Bedarf an Stauraum hinaus beschäftigten sich die Architekten ebenfalls mit den radikalen Veränderungen im Alltag, die ein Baby mit sich bringt. Wir alle haben schon einmal beobachtet, wie Babys alles, was sie erwischen, auf den Fußboden werfen, und die Erwachsenen alles wieder aufheben. Genau genommen machen die Architekten diese natürliche Gewohnheit sogar zum Verbündeten der Eltern, wodurch der Fußboden das ganze Durcheinander mit einigen Besenschwüngen einfach „schlucken" kann.

Au-delà du besoin de rangement, les architectes se sont également préoccupés des changements radicaux du quotidien qui accompagnent la naissance d'un enfant. Nous avons tous en tête l'image du bébé qui jette au sol tout ce qu'il peut attraper en attendant que les adultes ramassent ces objets. Les architectes ont transformé cette habitude en un allié des parents, en installant un plancher capable « d'avaler » tout le désordre en quelques coups de balai.

Más allá de la necesidad de tener almacenaje, los arquitectos también se preocuparon por los drásticos cambios que un bebé genera en el día a día. Todos hemos visto cómo los bebes lanzan cualquier cosa al suelo y es recogida por los adultos. Los arquitectos en realidad transforman este hábito natural en el aliado de los padres, permitiendo que el suelo "trague" todo este desorden con unas cuantas pasadas de escoba.

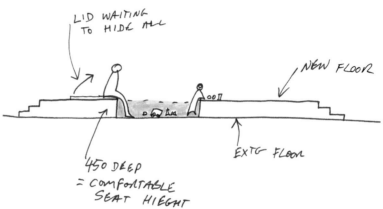

Conceptual diagrams

Not only is the floor an efficient storage space, but also, as the child grows older, it becomes a place for playing and hiding. The toy box is 45 centimetres deep, which actually is roughly the height of a seat. It makes for a play space at a comfortable seat height for adults.

Der Fußboden ist nicht nur ein effizienter Stauraum sondern wird, während das Kind heranwächst, auch ein Ort zum Spielen und Verstecken. Der Spielzeugkasten ist 45 Zentimeter tief, was eigentlich in etwa der Höhe eines Sitzes entspricht. So entsteht ein Spielbereich auf einer für Erwachsene bequemen Sitzhöhe.

Non seulement le sol est un espace de rangement judicieux, mais il est aussi un espace de jeu et de cachettes lorsque l'enfant grandit. Le coffre à jouets fait 45 centimètres de profondeur c'est-à-dire à peu près la hauteur du siège. Il s'agit donc d'un espace de jeu dont la hauteur est idéale pour que les adultes s'y assoient.

El suelo, además de ser un eficiente espacio de almacenaje se convertirá en un lugar de juegos y escondite cuando el niño sea mayor. La caja de juguetes tiene 45 centímetros de fondo, lo que equivale prácticamente a la altura de un asiento. Hace que el espacio de juegos sea un cómodo asiento para adultos.

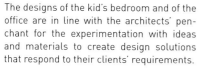

The designs of the kid's bedroom and of the office are in line with the architects' penchant for the experimentation with ideas and materials to create design solutions that respond to their clients' requirements.

Die Entwürfe für das Kinderschlafzimmer und das Büro stehen im Einklang mit der Neigung des Architekten, mit Ideen und Materialien zu experimentieren, um Designlösungen zu schaffen, die auf die Anforderungen seiner Kunden eingehen.

L'aménagement de la chambre d'enfant et du bureau cadre avec le goût des architectes pour l'expérimentation de nouvelles idées et l'utilisation de nouveaux matériaux dans le but de trouver des solutions pour répondre aux exigences de leurs clients.

El diseño de la habitación de los niños y de la oficina está en consonancia con el gusto de los arquitectos por la experimentación con ideas y materiales que permiten crear soluciones a los requerimientos de sus clientes.

70 m² // 753 sq ft

Photo © Beppe Giardino

FERMI // BLAARCHITETTI

TURIN, ITALY

The project involved an extensive renovation of an apartment in disrepair. While work had to be done around pre-existing structural walls, the layout and, more specifically, the provision for space-efficient storage is a successful solution for keeping the apartment clutter free.

Das Projekt umfasste die umfangreiche Renovierung einer baufälligen Wohnung. Während die Arbeiten um bereits bestehende Tragmauern erfolgen mussten, ist der Grundriss - genauer gesagt das Einplanen von platzsparendem Stauraum - eine erfolgreiche Lösung, um die Wohnung in einem aufgeräumten Zustand zu halten.

Ce projet impliquait la rénovation de grande envergure d'un appartement délabré. Alors que des travaux devaient être effectués autour des murs d'origine, l'agencement et, plus spécifiquement, la mise en place de rangements peu encombrants restait une solution efficace pour éviter que l'appartement ne soit trop chargé.

El proyecto implicaba una exhaustiva renovación de un apartamento en mal estado. En la renovación, se mantuvieron las paredes estructurales ya existentes, pero se modificó la distribución del espacio y, más específicamente, la disposición de lugares de almacenaje eficientes: una solución muy acertada para mantener el apartamento ordenado.

www.blaarchitettura.it // Project: Alberto Lessan and Jacopo Bracco | Project team: Cecilia Mauro | Energy project: Federico Cerutti

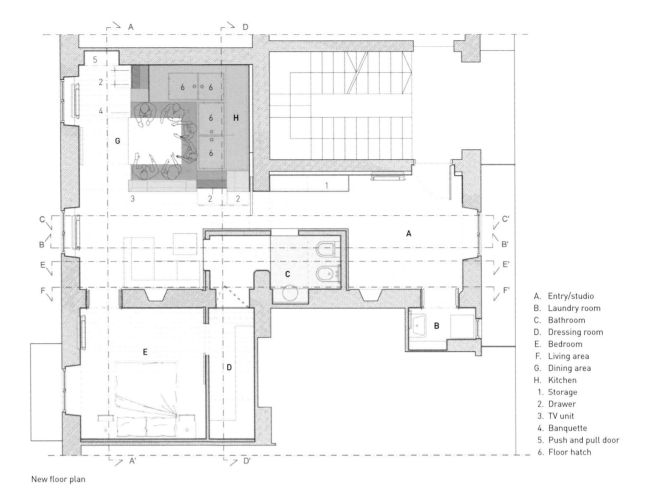

New floor plan

A. Entry/studio
B. Laundry room
C. Bathroom
D. Dressing room
E. Bedroom
F. Living area
G. Dining area
H. Kitchen
1. Storage
2. Drawer
3. TV unit
4. Banquette
5. Push and pull door
6. Floor hatch

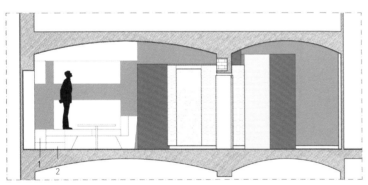

Section A

1. Push and pull door
2. Storage

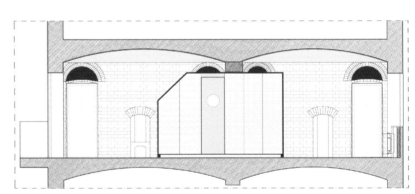

Section C

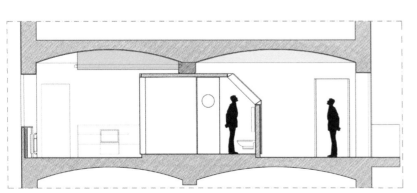

Section B

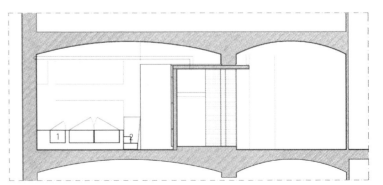

Section D

1. Floor hatch
2. Drawer

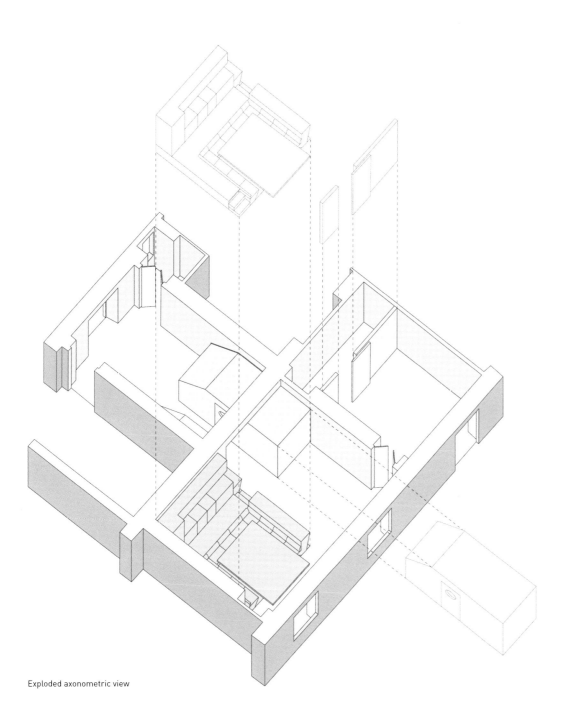

Exploded axonometric view

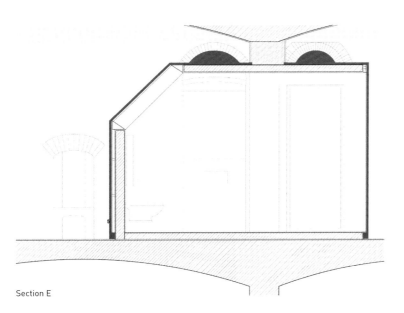

Section E

The kitchen concentrates high-density storage under a raised floor and compact equipment. The dining area is framed by open shelves and steps that double as storage benches.

Die Küche beherbergt Stauraum mit hoher Dichte unter einem Doppelboden und eine kompakte Ausstattung. Der Essbereich wird von offenen Regalen und Stufen umrahmt, die auch als Bänke mit Stauraum dienen.

La plupart des rangements de la cuisine sont concentrés sous un sol surélevé et dans l'équipement compact. Le coin-repas est encadré par des étagères et des marches qui servent également de lieu de stockage.

La cocina concentra mucho espacio de almacenaje, bajo el suelo elevado y en el equipamiento compacto. La zona de comedor se sitúa entre estanterías abiertas y escalones que actúan como bancos de almacenamiento.

Two steps lead to the kitchen, which wraps the dining area along two sides in an analogy to the main deck of a ship.

Zwei Stufen führen zur Küche, die den Essbereich an zwei Seiten in einer Analogie zum Hauptdeck eines Schiffs umschließt.

Deux marches mènent à la cuisine qui enveloppe la salle à manger des deux côtés pour évoquer le pont principal d'un bateau.

Dos escalones conducen a la cocina, que envuelve la zona de comedor por dos laterales, de una manera similar a la cubierta principal de un barco.

Near the entry, a wooden volume containing the bathroom separates the living area from the bedroom. The side facing the living area has an opening filled in with a frosted glass pane to make the wooden volume less obstructive.

In der Nähe des Eingangs trennt ein Gebilde aus Holz, in dem das Bad untergebracht ist, den Wohnbereich vom Schlafzimmer ab. Die dem Wohnbereich zugewandte Seite hat eine Öffnung, die mit Milchglas ausgefüllt ist, um dem Holzgebilde mehr Transparenz zu verleihen.

Près de l'entrée, un volume en bois contenant la salle de bains sépare le séjour de la chambre. Le côté opposé au séjour est ouvert par un panneau de verre dépoli afin que la partie en bois ressorte moins.

Junto a la entrada, un volumen de madera que alberga el baño separa la zona de estar del dormitorio. Para hacer que este volumen de madera fuese más ligero, en el lateral junto a la zona de estar tiene una abertura cubierta con un recuadro de cristal esmerilado.

35 m² // 377 sq ft

Photo © Francesco Russo

STUDIO FLAT // CREATIVE IDEAS & ARCHITECTURE OFFICE
LONDON, UNITED KINGDOM

The renovation of a 35-square-meter studio flat responds to the client's request for the creation of a compact living space where he could live comfortably even when his family and friends are visiting, without having to compromise on space. The open plan layout eliminates unnecessary boundaries, allowing light to flow inside.

Die Renovierung dieses 35 Quadratmeter großen Studios berücksichtigt den Wunsch des Kunden, einen kompakten Wohnraum zu schaffen, in dem er, selbst wenn Familie und Freunde zu Besuch kommen, komfortabel leben kann, ohne sich im Platz einschränken zu müssen. Die offene Gestaltung beseitigt unnötige Begrenzungen und lässt das Licht ungehindert nach innen fallen.

La rénovation de ce studio de 35 m² répond à la demande du client : il fallait créer un espace de vie compact, où il pourrait vivre confortablement même lors de visites de sa famille et de ses amis, sans faire de compromis sur l'espace. L'agencement décloisonné élimine des frontières superflues, ce qui permet à la lumière de pénétrer à l'intérieur.

La renovación de un estudio de 35 m² responde a la solicitud del cliente de crear un espacio habitable y compacto donde poder vivir cómodamente incluso cuando su familia y amigos lo visitaran, sin que el propio espacio fuera un inconveniente. La disposición abierta del plano elimina los límites innecesarios, permitiendo que la luz fluya en su interior.

www.ciao.archi // Team: Diego Dalpra, Enrico Less, Alessandro Penna, Tiberia Motoc, Francesco Russo, and Guido Morello

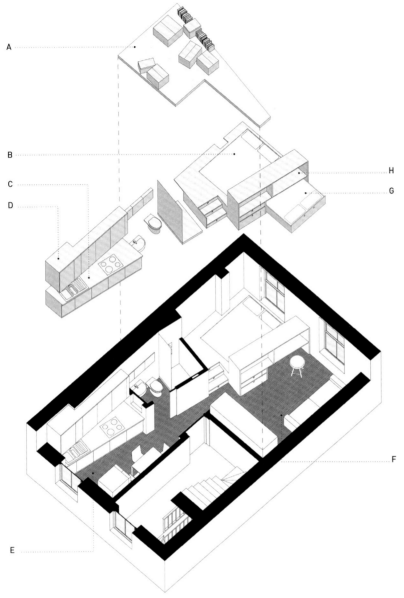

Exploded axonometric view

A. Mezzanine/Storage   E. Bolon flooring
B. Main double bed   F. Under floor heating
C. Bespoke kitchen furniture   G. Secondary double bed
D. Boiler   H. Desk

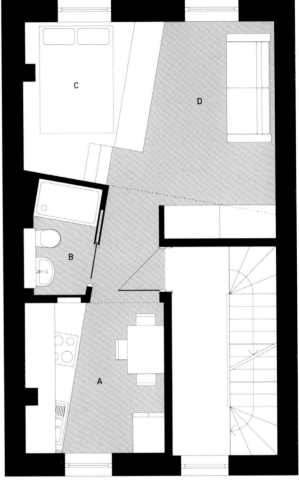

Floor plan

A. Kitchen/dining
B. Bathroom
C. Bedroom/storage
D. Living/office

Part of the floor is raised to accommodate the bed. It is separated from the living area by a bookshelf that has its back lined with felt to optimise acoustic comfort. Extra storage space is provided by the built-in wardrobe in the living area and the drawers within the steps leading to the raised bed and to a storage space above the bathroom.

Ein Teil des Bodens ist erhöht, um dort das Bett unterzubringen. Es wird vom Wohnbereich durch ein Bücherregal abgetrennt, dessen Rückseite mit Filz ausgekleidet ist, um den akustischen Komfort zu optimieren. Zusätzlicher Stauraum wird durch den Einbaukleiderschrank im Wohnbereich und die Schubfächer in den Stufen, die zu dem Hochbett und einem Stauraum über dem Bad führen, bereitgestellt.

Une partie du sol est surélevée pour accueillir le lit. Celui-ci est séparé de l'espace de vie par une bibliothèque dont le dos est recouvert de feutre pour un confort acoustique optimal. De l'espace de rangement supplémentaire est apporté par le dressing intégré dans la pièce de vie et par des tiroirs encastrés à l'intérieur des marches menant au lit en mezzanine. Un espace de stockage se situe au-dessus de la salle de bains.

Parte del suelo se eleva para dar cabida a la cama. Está separada del salón por una estantería forrada con fieltro en la parte posterior, para optimizar el confort acústico. Se proporciona espacio de almacenamiento adicional a través del armario empotrado del salón y de los cajones de los escalones que conducen a la cama. También hay un espacio de almacenamiento encima del baño.

The bespoke furniture adapts to space and function. Such is the case of a second bed neatly hidden under the raised floor. When not used, the second bed leaves space to a clever home office.

Die maßgeschneiderten Möbel passen sich an Raum und Funktion an. Ebenso wie das zweite Bett, das geschickt unter dem Doppelboden verborgen ist. Wird es gerade nicht benutzt, schafft das zweite Bett Platz für ein pfiffiges Home Office.

Le mobilier sur mesure s'adapte en fonction de l'espace et des besoins des habitants. C'est le cas d'un deuxième lit dissimulé sous la surélévation. Lorsqu'il ne sert pas, il laisse place à un ingénieux bureau.

El mobiliario a medida se adapta espacial y funcionalmente. Como es el caso de una segunda cama cuidadosamente escondida bajo el suelo elevado. Cuando no se utiliza, la segunda cama deja espacio para una ingeniosa oficina en casa.

Despite its small dimensions, the kitchen looks spacious. The lack of pulls or handles on the cabinet fronts and the light colour scheme contribute to this effect.

Trotz ihrer geringen Dimensionen wirkt die Küche geräumig. Das Fehlen von Knöpfen bzw. Griffen an den Schrankfronten und das helle Farbschema kommen diesem Effekt zugute.

Malgré ses petites dimensions, la cuisine a l'air spacieuse. L'absence de poignées ou de tirettes sur les placards et l'utilisation d'une palette de couleurs claires contribuent à cet effet.

A pesar de sus pequeñas dimensiones, la cocina parece espaciosa. La falta de tiradores o picaportes en los frentes del armario y la paleta de colores claros, contribuyen a crear este efecto.

25 m² // 266 sq ft

Photo © Hazel Yuen Fun, Dennis Cheung

KOWLOON BAY // DESIGN EIGHT FIVE TWO

HONG KONG, SAR CHINA

The design sought to create the same comfort and feeling of spaciousness to which people are accustomed in larger homes, while optimising the use of the space available. The apartment is more akin to the image of the bachelor pad, compact, functional, but easy to maintain.

Der Entwurf bemühte sich um den gleichen Komfort und das Gefühl von Geräumigkeit, an das Menschen in größeren Häusern gewöhnt sind, bei gleichzeitiger Optimierung des zur Verfügung stehenden Raumes. Die Wohnung ähnelt eher einer Junggesellenbude: Kompakt und funktionell, doch pflegeleicht.

Le concept était de créer la même impression de confort et d'espace que celle éprouvée par les personnes habituées à vivre dans des habitations plus grandes, tout en optimisant l'utilisation de l'espace disponible. Cet appartement s'apparente plutôt à l'image que l'on se fait de la « garçonnière », étant compact, fonctionnel, mais facile d'entretien.

Con este diseño se buscó crear el confort y la sensación de amplitud que sentimos en viviendas más grandes, a la vez que se optimiza el espacio disponible. El apartamento se asemeja más a un piso de soltero: compacto, funcional y de fácil mantenimiento.

www.designeightfivetwo.com // Team: Norman Ung, Peter Lampard, Ryan Lam, Hazel Fun Yuen, and Tony Lai

Floor plan. Dining table as desk

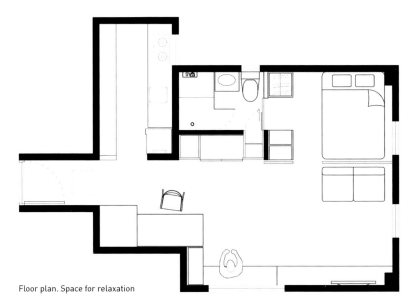

Floor plan. Space for relaxation

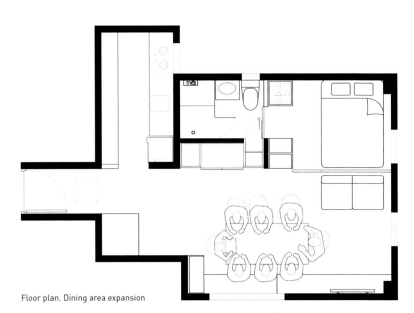

Floor plan. Dining area expansion

Floor plan. Home theatre

A raised platform accommodates the bed, complete with storage beneath. This type of bed, also known as captain's bed, takes cue from the beds used on board ships, where space is valuable and a regular bed is impractical.

Eine erhöhte Plattform beherbergt das Bett samt Stauraum darunter. Diese Art von Bett, alias Kapitänsbett, ließ sich von den Betten inspirieren, die an Bord von Schiffen benutzt werden, wo der Platz wertvoll und ein normales Bett unpraktisch ist.

Une plateforme surélevée accueille le lit sous lequel se trouvent des espaces de rangement. Ce type de lit, que l'on appelle aussi « lit capitaine », s'inspire des lits installés sur les bateaux, où l'espace est précieux et un lit normal peu pratique.

En una plataforma elevada se encuentra la cama, que contiene espacio de almacenamiento en su interior. Este tipo de cama tiene su origen en los camarotes de los capitanes de barcos, donde el espacio es valioso y una cama tradicional poco práctica.

The home integrates the very best aspects of small spaces with Hong Kong history. All furnishings have multiple uses highlighting the apartment's proportions, while modernizing and opening up the living and entertaining areas.

Diese Wohnung verknüpft die allerbesten Aspekte kleiner Räume mit der Geschichte Hong Kongs. Alle Einrichtungsgegenstände haben mehrere Verwendungszwecke, welche die Proportionen der Wohnung hervorheben, während Wohn- und Empfangsbereich modernisiert und erschlossen werden.

Cette maison entre dans l'histoire de Hong Kong pour avoir su parfaitement adapter l'aménagement intérieur à un espace réduit. Tout le mobilier a de multiples usages qui soulignent les proportions de l'intérieur tout en modernisant et ouvrant les pièces de vie et de réception.

La casa integra lo mejor de los espacios pequeños con la historia de Hong Kong. Todo el mobiliario tiene múltiples usos destacando las proporciones del apartamento, y al mismo tiempo modernizándolo y abriéndolo a las zonas comunes y de ocio.

© João Morgado

A GRAPHIC REFURBISHMENT BY THE SEA // TIAGO DO VALE ARQUITECTOS

CAMINHA, PORTUGAL

An out-dated apartment was in need of a substantial remodel. The owner had two requests when he approached the design team: the original layout had to be maintained, and the costs be kept down. Such a clear brief set the tone for a strong concept that materialized into brightly coloured wall panels.

Diese veraltete Wohnung benötigte eine umfangreiche Umgestaltung. Der Besitzer hatte zwei Wünsche, als er auf das Designteam zuging: Der ursprüngliche Grundriss sollte beibehalten und die Kosten niedrig gehalten werden. Eine derart klare Anweisung gab den Ton für ein starkes Konzept an, das in Form von farbenfrohen Wandpaneelen Gestalt annahm.

Cet appartement vieillot avait besoin d'un remaniement conséquent. Le propriétaire avait deux souhaits lorsqu'il a contacté l'équipe d'architectes : conserver l'agencement d'origine, et que cela ne soit pas hors de prix. Avec ces instructions claires, le ton était donné pour un concept fort qui s'est concrétisé par des panneaux aux couleurs vives.

Este apartamento anticuado necesitaba una extensa remodelación. El dueño tenía dos peticiones para el equipo de diseño: la configuración original debía mantenerse y los costes debían ser mínimos. Estos requisitos tan claros marcaron la pauta que posteriormente se materializó en paneles de pared de vivos colores.

www.tiagodovale.com // Team: Tiago do Vale, María Cainzos Osinde, Hugo Quintela, and Louane Papin

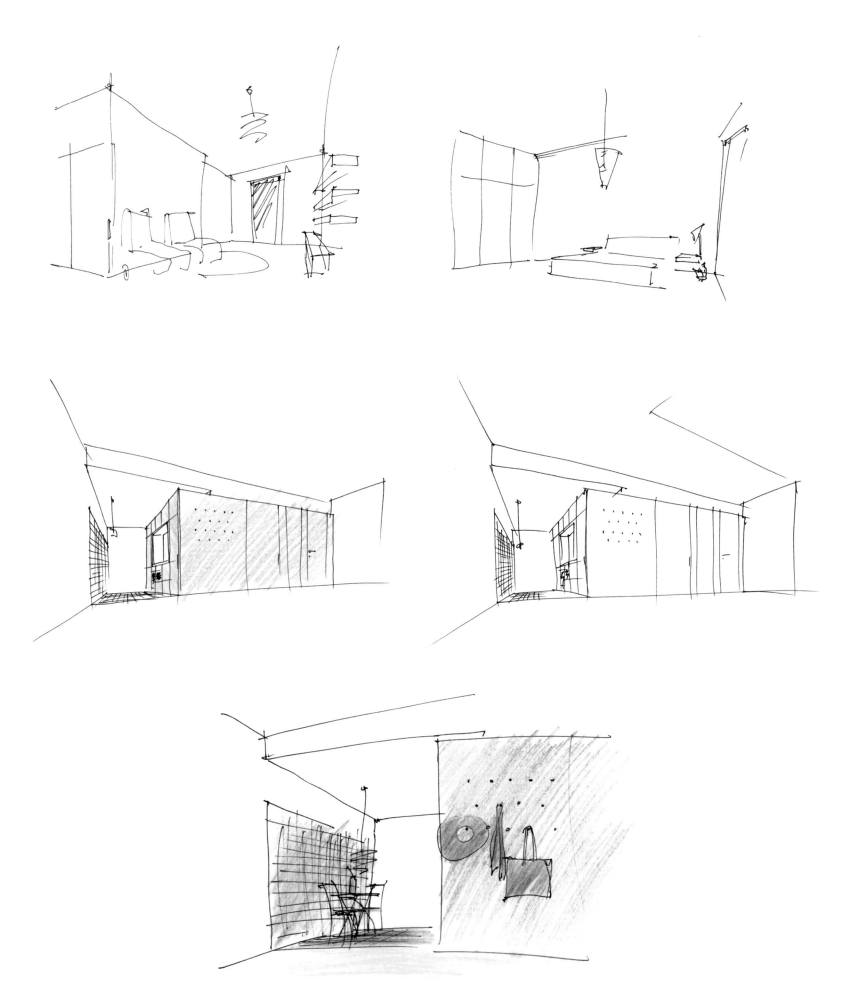

Design development sketches

Floor plan

Section C1

Section C2

Section C3

Section C4

Section 5

Section C6

Section 7

Section C8

Section C9

Section 9 (closed doors)

Bright blue panels cover the wall outside the bathroom, integrating the entry door, and the bathroom door. The blue panels then turn the corner to become the kitchen's cabinet fronts.

Hellblaue Paneele bedecken die Wand vor dem Badezimmer und integrieren Eingangs- und Badezimmertür. Die blauen Verkleidungen biegen dann um die Ecke, um zu Küchenschrankfronten zu werden.

Des panneaux bleu vif couvrent le mur extérieur de la salle de bains, intégrant la porte d'entrée et la porte de la salle de bains. Ils suivent ensuite l'angle du mur pour devenir les façades du placard de la cuisine.

Los paneles azules cubren la pared exterior del baño, integrando la puerta de entrada y la del baño. Después, los paneles azules giran y se convierten en los muebles de la cocina.

The blue panels also offer the opportunity for a playful arrangement of hooks that enliven the entry hall.

Die blauen Verkleidungen bieten auch die Möglichkeit für eine spielerische Anordnung von Haken, welche die Empfangshalle beleben.

Ces panneaux bleus permettent également de placer de manière ludique des crochets qui donnent vie au hall d'entrée.

Los paneles azules también permiten una divertida disposición de colgadores que dan vida a la entrada.

Part of the wall between the living area and the bedroom is a sliding panel. When closed, it allows for a clear separation between the two areas, satisfying the need for privacy. When opened, the two areas fuse in a continuous open space.

Ein Teil der Wand zwischen Wohnbereich und Schlafzimmer ist eine Schiebewand. Wenn sie geschlossen ist, sorgt sie für eine klare Trennung zwischen den beiden Bereichen und wird dem Bedarf an Privatleben gerecht. Wenn sie geöffnet ist, verschmelzen beide Bereiche in einem durchgehenden offenen Raum.

Une partie du mur entre la pièce de vie et la chambre est un panneau coulissant. Lorsqu'il est fermé, il permet une séparation nette entre les deux espaces, ce qui répond au besoin d'intimité. Lorsqu'il est ouvert, les deux zones fusionnent en un grand espace continu.

Parte de la pared entre la zona de estar y el dormitorio es un panel deslizante. Cuando se cierra, se separan nítidamente las dos áreas, cumpliendo así la necesidad de privacidad. Cuando se abre, las dos áreas se funden en un espacio abierto contínuo.

27 m² // 291 sq ft

Photo © Katherine Lu

THE STUDIO // NICHOLAS GURNEY

SYDNEY, NEW SOUTH WALES, AUSTRALIA

A wooden "pod" was inserted into an open space to address the issues of privacy, storage and a lack of living space inherent to small apartments. The low cost and sturdy structure features full height, wall-to-wall sliding doors, and accommodates an entry foyer, storage, washing and sleeping zones.

Eine hölzerne „Hülse" wurde in einen offenen Raum eingesetzt, um die Themen Privatleben, Stauraum und Mangel an Wohnfläche anzugehen, die für kleine Wohnungen so typisch sind. Die kostengünstige und stabile Struktur besteht aus Schiebetüren in voller Höhe, die von Wand zu Wand reichen, und umfasst Eingangsfoyer, Stauraum sowie Wasch- und Schlafbereiche.

Une construction en bois a été insérée dans un espace décloisonné pour répondre aux besoins d'intimité, de rangement et au manque d'espace de vie inhérent aux petits appartements. Sa structure peu chère et robuste comporte des portes coulissantes de mur à mur, et accueille un foyer d'entrée, du rangement, et des zones dédiées à la toilette ou au couchage.

Los apartamentos pequeños suelen carecer de espacio de almacenamiento, zona de estar e, incluso, privacidad. Para dar respuesta a estos problemas inherentes a los pequeños espacios, en este proyecto se usó un "contenedor" de madera. Esta robusta estructura de bajo coste se caracteriza por su altura completa, puertas correderas de lado a lado y por albergar una entrada, zona de almacenamiento, dormitorio y zona de aseo.

www.nicholasgurney.com.au // Team: Nicholas Gurney

The open quality of the space provides an adequate setup for flexible use, while ingenious storage solutions keep the home tidy and organized.

Die offene Natur des Raumes bietet eine passende Einrichtung für den flexiblen Einsatz, während geniale Stauraumlösungen dafür sorgen, dass die Wohnung aufgeräumt und geordnet wirkt.

L'espace décloisonné permet une installation et une utilisation flexible de ce nouvel habitat tandis que des solutions de rangement ingénieuses maintiennent ordre et organisation dans la maison.

Al ser un espacio abierto proporciona una configuración adecuada para un uso flexible. Además, las ingeniosas soluciones de almacenaje mantienen la vivienda recogida y organizada.

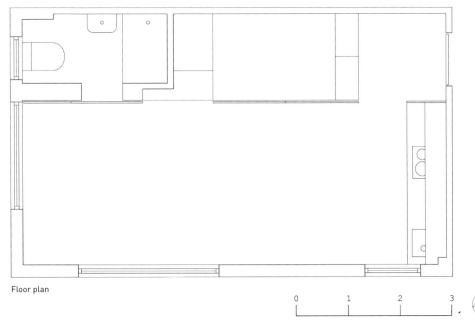

Floor plan

0   1   2   3

The design of the kitchen block appears as an extension of the pod. Inner workings are totally concealed. Space limitations discouraged the use of conventional kitchen drawers.

Das Design des Küchenblocks scheint eine Erweiterung der Hülse zu sein. Die Funktionen sind im Inneren total verborgen. Platzbeschränkungen sprachen gegen den Einsatz herkömmlicher Küchenschubladen.

La conception du bloc cuisine apparaît comme une extension de la construction en bois. Les mécanismes internes sont complètement masqués. L'espace limité a empêché l'installation de tiroirs de cuisine conventionnels.

Por su diseño, el módulo de la cocina parece una extensión del contenedor. El funcionamiento interno está completamente oculto. Se evitó el uso de los tradicionales cajones de cocina por la limitación de espacio.

KERAMOS // ADRIANO DESIGN FOR COPRODOTTO

www.adrianodesign.it

Keramos is a modular container in ceramic characterised with an innovative binding system made of wood, which allows vertical and horizontal configurations. The materiality, the proportions, the colours and the high-gloss finish of the ceramic makes Keramos a unique piece of furniture.

Keramos ist ein modularer Behälter aus Keramik, geprägt durch ein innovatives Verbindungssystem aus Holz, das vertikale und horizontale Konfigurationen ermöglicht. Die Stofflichkeit, Proportionen, Farben und Hochglanzoberfläche der Keramik machen Keramos zu einem einzigartigen Möbelstück.

Keramos est un meuble modulaire en céramique caractérisé par un système novateur en bois qui permet des configurations verticales comme horizontales. L'adaptabilité, les proportions, les couleurs et la finition ultra brillante de la céramique font de Keramos un meuble unique.

Keramos es un contenedor modular de cerámica que se caracteriza por un novedoso sistema de cierre en madera. Puede usarse tanto vertical como horizontalmente. El material, las proporciones, los colores y el acabado brillante de la cerámica hacen de Keramos una pieza de mobiliario única.

Manufacturer: CoProdotto // www.coprodotto.it
Materials: ceramic shells, wooden seaming,

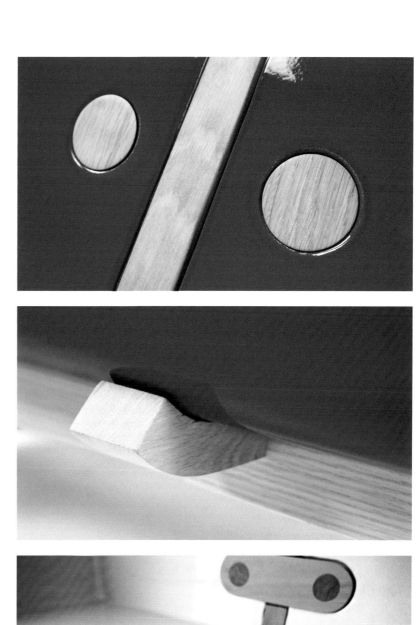

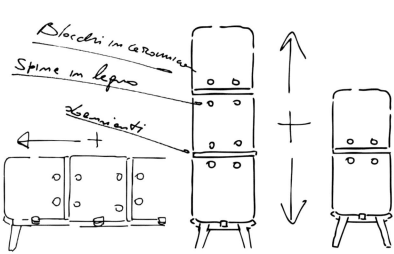

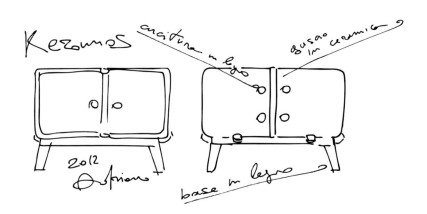

Conceptual design sketches

The distinctive line of Keramos cabinets reminds one of the large ceramic vessels used in ancient history for the transportation and preservation of goods.

Die markante Linie der Keramos-Schränke erinnert an die großen Keramikgefäße, die in früheren Zeiten für den Transport und die Aufbewahrung von Waren verwendet wurden.

La ligne distinctive des vitrines Keramos rappelle les grands récipients en céramique utilisés dans l'Antiquité pour le transport et la conservation de marchandises.

La característica línea de armarios de Keramos recuerda a las grandes vasijas cerámicas usadas en la antigüedad para el transporte y conservación de productos.

Keramos is a multi-award winning product that embodies the expertise and the finesse of Italian craftsmanship in the production of ceramic products.

Keramos ist ein mehrfach ausgezeichnetes Produkt, das die Kompetenz und Finesse der italienischen Handwerkskunst bei der Herstellung von Keramikprodukten verkörpert.

Keramos est un produit récompensé par de nombreux prix qui personnifie l'expertise et la finesse du savoir-faire italien dans la fabrication de produits en céramique.

Keramos, un producto galardonado varias veces, reúne la experiencia y el gusto de los artesanos italianos por la elaboración de objetos de cerámica.

78 m² // 840 sq ft

LEVENT HOUSE // COA MIMARLIK
ISTANBUL, TURKEY

The apartment was designed for a newly married couple. It was important for the designers to understand the design taste, needs, and lifestyles of the users of the apartment, both as a couple and as individuals. In order to better address each of the requirements, the designers encouraged their clients to engage in the design process.

Die Wohnung wurde für ein frisch verheiratetes Paar konzipiert. Für die Gestalter war es wichtig, den Designgeschmack, die Bedürfnisse und den Lebensstil der Benutzer der Wohnung - als Paar und als Einzelpersonen - zu verstehen. Um den jeweiligen Anforderungen besser gerecht zu werden, ermutigten die Gestalter ihre Kunden, sich am Designprozess zu beteiligen.

Cet appartement a été conçu pour un couple de jeunes mariés. Il était important pour les concepteurs de comprendre le goût, les besoins ainsi que le style de vie des usagers de l'appartement, en tant que couple mais aussi en tant qu'individus. Afin de mieux répondre à chaque exigence, ils ont encouragé leurs clients à s'impliquer dans le processus de création.

El apartamento se diseñó para una pareja recién casada. Para los diseñadores era importante entender el gusto, las necesidades y el estilo de vida de los habitantes, como pareja e individualmente. Con el fin responder mejor a cada uno de los requisitos, los diseñadores animaron a los clientes a implicarse en el proceso de diseño.

www.coamimarlik.com // Team: Cihan Atliman and Özlem Güler Atliman

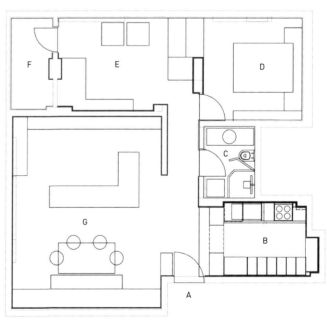

Floor plan

A. Entrance   E. Office
B. Kitchen   F. Balcony
C. Bathroom   G. Living room
D. Bedroom

The design of the bookshelf in the living room is a collaborative effort between the clients and the designers. The lower cabinets and the vertical white structures are fixed, while the location of shelves and white boxes can be changed.

Der Entwurf für das Bücherregal im Wohnzimmer ist eine gemeinsame Arbeit von Kunden und Designern. Die unteren Schränke und die vertikalen weißen Strukturen sind fest, während die Position der Regale und der weißen Kästen verändert werden kann.

Le design de cette bibliothèque est le fruit d'un travail collaboratif entre les clients et les concepteurs. Les placards bas et les structures verticales blanches sont fixes, tandis que les étagères et les modules blancs peuvent changer de place.

El diseño de la librería de la sala de estar es fruto del trabajo en equipo entre los clientes y los diseñadores. Los armarios inferiores y las blancas estructuras verticales están fijas, mientras que la ubicación de las estanterías y las cajas blancas se puede cambiar.

LA CUCINA

34 m² // 366 sq ft

Photo © Orlando Gutiérrez

MODULOR / ZOOCO ESTUDIO

MADRID, SPAIN

The design comprises a series of porticoes organized according to daily activities. Sleep, work, play, wash and dress. The design addresses the need to organize the home based on an orderly sequence of daily routines.

Der Entwurf umfasst eine Reihe von Portiken, die den täglichen Aktivitäten entsprechend angeordnet sind. Schlafen, arbeiten, spielen, waschen und ankleiden. Die Gestaltung befasst sich mit der Notwendigkeit, das Zuhause basierend auf einer geordneten Abfolge der Tagesabläufe anzuordnen.

L'agencement intérieur de cet appartement comprend une série de portiques organisés en fonction des activités quotidiennes : dormir, travailler, jouer, se laver et s'habiller. Le concept répond au besoin d'organiser la maison à partir d'une séquence ordonnée de routines quotidiennes.

El diseño reúne una serie de pórticos modulares organizados según las actividades diarias: dormir, trabajar, jugar, asearse y vestirse. El diseño hace hincapié en la necesidad de organizar la vivienda basándose en una ordenada secuencia de rutinas diarias.

www.zooco.es // Team: Miguel Crespo Picot and Javier Guzmán Benito

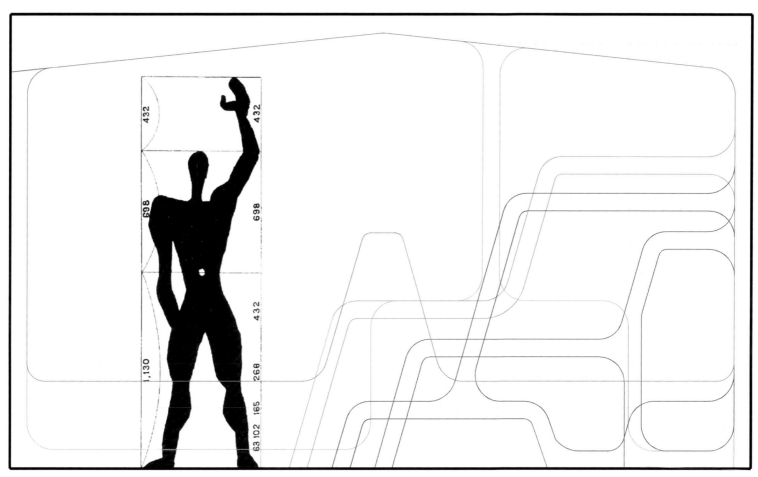

Section

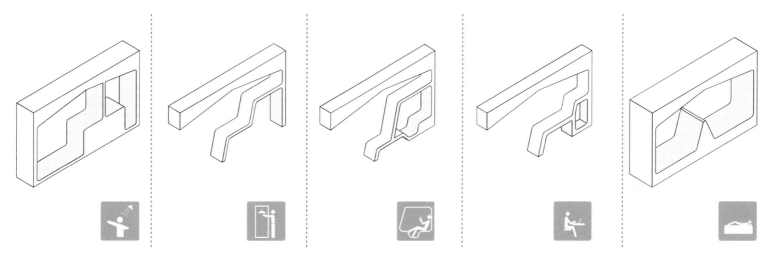

Functional diagram

Just as its name suggests, the project pays tribute to the measurement system Modulor created by Le Corbusier with the same name in the 60s. The design also takes cue from Leonardo Da Vinci's Vitruvian Man, an illustration that expresses his theories on proportion.

Wie der Name schon sagt, würdigt das Projekt das von Le Corbusier in den Sechziger Jahren kreierte gleichnamige Proportionssystem Modulor. Das Design nimmt auch Leonardo da Vincis vitruvianische Figur als Vorbild, eine Abbildung, die dessen Theorien zu Proportionen zum Ausdruck bringt.

Comme son nom le suggère, ce projet est un hommage au système de mesure Modulor créé par Le Corbusier dans les années 1940. Le concept s'inspire également de l'homme de Vitruve dessiné par Léonard de Vinci où figurent ses théories sur la proportion.

Como su nombre indica, el proyecto rinde tributo al sistema de medidas Modulor creado por Le Corbusier con este nombre en los 60. El diseño también se vincula con el Hombre de Vitruvio de Leonardo Da Vinci, una ilustración que muestra su teoría sobre las proporciones.

Different colours are associated to the different areas of the space following the chromotherapy guidelines.

Unter Einhaltung der Vorgaben der Farbtherapie werden unterschiedliche Farben verschiedenen Bereichen des Raumes zugeordnet.

Différentes couleurs sont associées à différentes zones de l'espace en suivant les principes de la chromothérapie.

Los distintos colores se asocian con diferentes áreas del espacio siguiendo las directrices de la cromoterapia.

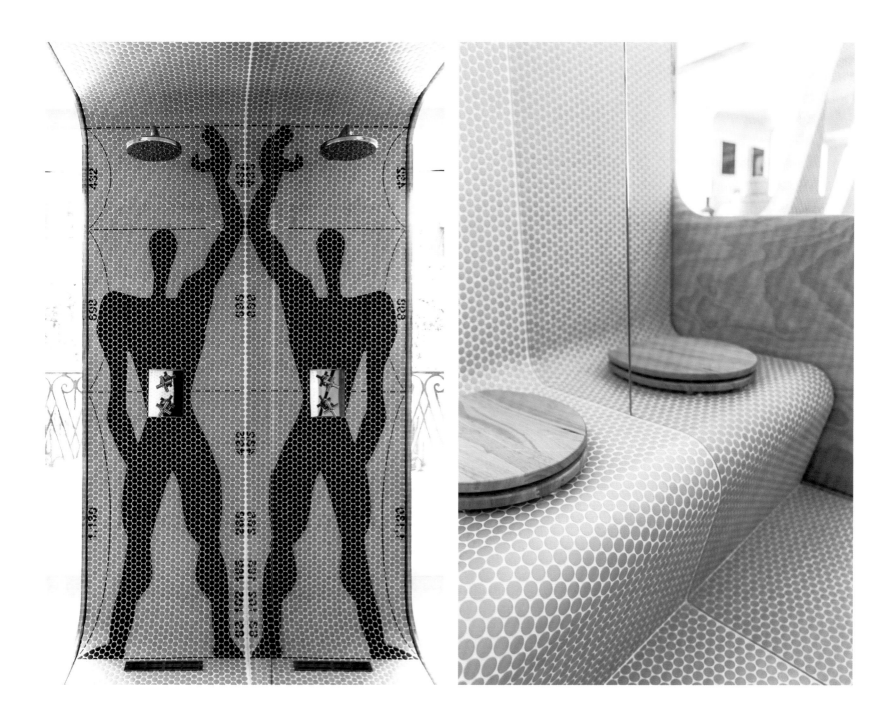

106 m² // 1,140 sq ft

THE GRID // COUDAMY ARCHITECTURES
PARIS, FRANCE

The main priority in the redesign of this apartment was the creation of an open space that would integrate high-density storage. A metallic modular cubic structure demarcates the different areas of the living area, while integrating a personalized composition of open and closed storage formed by white and natural bamboo cubes.

Die Hauptpriorität bei der Neugestaltung dieser Wohnung war die Schaffung eines offenen Raumes, der einen Stauraum hoher Dichte integrieren würde. Eine modulare Würfelstruktur aus Metall begrenzt die unterschiedlichen Bereiche des Wohnbereichs und integriert gleichzeitig eine individuell gestaltete Komposition aus offenem und geschlossenem Stauraum, der aus Würfeln in Weiß und aus echtem Bambus besteht.

La priorité principale lors du remaniement de cet appartement était de créer un espace ouvert qui intégrerait un rangement de grande capacité. Une structure de cubes métalliques modulables fait la démarcation entre les différentes zones de la pièce à vivre. Les cubes, ouverts ou fermés, blancs ou en bambou, sont agencés de manière personnalisée et constituent autant de solutions de rangement.

La principal prioridad existente en el rediseño de este apartamento fue la creación de un espacio abierto que incluyera muchas opciones de almacenamiento. Una estructura cúbica, metálica y modular delimita las diferentes áreas del salón, a la vez que se integra una composición personalizada de almacenamiento abierto y cerrado formada por cubos blancos de bambú natural.

www.coudamyarchitectures.com // Design by Paul Coudamy

Far from being obstructive, the aerial structure enhances the open character of the apartment. It delimits the different areas effortlessly, while offering interesting sightlines.

Weit davon entfernt hinderlich zu sein, beton die Luftstruktur den offenen Charakter der Wohnung. Sie begrenzt die unterschiedlichen Bereiche mühelos und bietet gleichzeitig interessante Sichtlinien.

Loin d'être gênante, la structure aérienne souligne le caractère décloisonné de l'appartement. Elle délimite les différentes zones sans effort, tout en offrant des perspectives intéressantes.

Lejos de ser un obstáculo, la estructura aérea mejora el carácter abierto del apartamento. Delimita las diferentes áreas fácilmente, a la vez que ofrece líneas de visión interesantes.

The modular design of the structure allows for a flexible organization of the space according to the needs of its occupants. It also incorporates the kitchen equipment, contributing to an integrated overall design of the living area.

Die modulare Bauweise der Struktur ermöglicht eine flexible Gestaltung des Raumes entsprechend den Bedürfnissen seiner Bewohner. Sie umfasst auch die Küchenausstattung und trägt so zu einer integrierten Gesamtgestaltung des Wohnbereichs bei.

Cette structure modulable permet de réorganiser facilement l'espace au gré des besoins de ses occupants. Elle intègre également une cuisine équipée, contribuant à l'ameublement total de la pièce à vivre.

El diseño modular de la estructura permite una organización flexible del espacio acorde a las necesidades de sus habitantes. Incorpora igualmente el equipamiento de la cocina, contribuyendo a un diseño totalmente integrado del salón.

The central space connecting the living areas and the bedrooms is called "The Moon". It is a large suspended disk emitting a diffused moon-like light that harmonizes with the shadows of the grid structure cast on the wall and ceiling of the apartment.

Der zentrale Raum, der die Wohnbereiche und Schlafzimmer verbindet, heißt „Der Mond", hierbei handelt es sich um eine große hängende Scheibe, die ein diffuses mondähnliches Licht ausstrahlt, das mit dem Schatten der Gitterstruktur harmonisiert, der an Wand und Decke der Wohnung geworfen wird.

L'espace central qui fait le lien entre les pièces à vivre et les chambres est appelé « La Lune ». C'est un grand disque suspendu qui émet une lumière diffuse évoquant celle de la Lune, s'harmonisant avec les ombres de la structure modulable projetées sur le mur et le plafond de l'appartement.

El espacio central llamado "La Luna", conecta las zonas de estar y las habitaciones. Es un disco grande suspendido que emite una luz difusa similar a la de la luna, en sintonía con las sombras de la estructura de rejilla de la pared y el techo del apartamento.

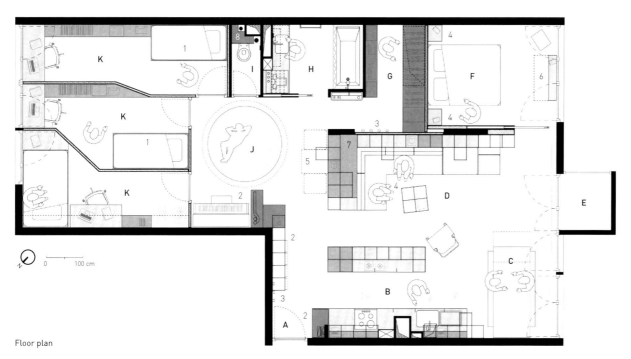

Floor plan

A. Entry
B. Kitchen
C. Dining area
D. Living area
E. Balcony
F. Master bedroom
G. Dressing room
H. Bathroom
I. Toilet room
J. "The Moon"
K. Bedroom

1. Storage box
   under the box
2. Open storage
3. Hangers
4. Drawer
5. Foldaway games
   table
6. Foldaway desk
7. HIFI/projector/
   CD storage
8. Storage for
   cleaning supplies

0   100 cm

380 m² // 4,090 sq ft

VILLA INTERIOR // BEEF ARCHITEKTI

PRAGUE, CZECH REPUBLIC

The original layout of this 90´s home was not taking full advantage of its large spaces and high ceilings. After opening it up, a large stone-clad volume integrating a fireplace was introduced as the centre of the house, around which all the functions are organized.

Der ursprüngliche Grundriss dieser Wohnstätte aus den neunziger Jahren nutzte die großen Räume und die hohen Decken nicht in vollem Umfang. Nach dessen Erschließung wurde ein großes mit Steinen verkleidetes Volumen, das einen Kamin einbindet, als Zentrum des Hauses geschaffen, um das sich alle Funktionen anordnen.

L'agencement premier de ce logement des années 1990 ne permettait pas de profiter pleinement de la totalité des espaces et des hauts plafonds. Après avoir ouvert l'ensemble, on y a introduit un épais mur en pierre, intégrant une cheminée, au centre de la maison, autour duquel s'organisent les différents lieux de vie.

El diseño original de esta casa de los años 90 no aprovechaba al máximo los amplios espacios y techos altos que tenía. El espacio se abrió y se introdujo un gran volumen revestido de piedra que integra una chimenea convertida en el centro de la casa, alrededor de la cual se organizan todas las funcionalidades de la misma.

www.beef.sk // Team: Radoslav Buzinkay, Andrej Ferenčík, and Jakub Viskupič

A floor-to-ceiling bookcase separates the media room from the main living space, while allowing visual connection between the two areas. The transparent character of the bookcase contrasts with the massiveness of the stone partition that integrates the fireplace.

Ein raumhohes Bücherregal trennt den Medienraum vom Hauptwohnbereich und ermöglicht gleichzeitig eine visuelle Verbindung zwischen den beiden Bereichen. Der transparente Charakter des Bücherregals steht in Kontrast zur Massivität der Steintrennwand, in die der Kamin eingelassen ist.

Une bibliothèque qui s'étire du sol au plafond sépare le salon vidéo-détente de la pièce de vie centrale, tout en permettant une connexion visuelle entre les deux. Le caractère ouvert de ce meuble contraste avec l'aspect massif de la cloison en pierre contenant la cheminée.

Una librería de suelo a techo separa la zona de televisión de la zona principal del salón, permitiendo la conexión visual entre ambas. El carácter abierto de la librería contrasta con la gran masa de piedra que forma parte de la chimenea.

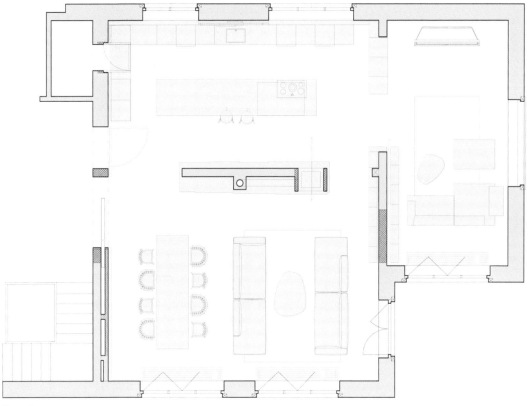

Floor plan

While lack of space was not an issue, the kitchen has under counter compact appliances and cupboards to maximize workspace. Additional storage was provided between the windows, meticulously designed to integrate a spice rack, cubbies glassware, a knife block, and a cutting board.

Obwohl Platzmangel hier kein Thema war, hat diese Küche kompakte Untertischgeräte und -schränke, um den Arbeitsbereich zu maximieren. Der Planer bietet zwischen den Fenstern zusätzlichen Stauraum, der sorgfältig entworfen wurde, und ein Gewürzregal, eine Gläserablage, einen Messerblock und ein Schneidebrett.

Bien qu'elle ne manque pas de volume, la cuisine a été optimisée à l'aide de placards et d'appareils ménagers encastrés sous le comptoir. Des espaces de rangement supplémentaire ont été ajoutés entre les fenêtres, conçus avec soin pour intégrer une étagère à épices, des étagères pour les verres, un bloc pour les couteaux et une planche à découper.

Al no haber falta de espacio, la cocina tiene los electrodomésticos y armarios bajo la encimera, para maximizar la zona de trabajo. Se habilitó almacenaje extra entre las ventanas, fruto de un diseño muy meticuloso que albergaba un pequeño estante de especias, espacios para la cristalería, un bloque para cuchillos y una tabla de cortar.

Kitchen cabinet view

35 m² // 377 sq ft

WORKROOM ARCHITECTS // RUETEMPLE

MOSCOW, RUSSIA

A stimulating environment is capable of promoting creativity. This is what might have thought the owner of this former garage when he gave it to his daughter, an architecture student. A unique single piece of furniture is the focus of the transformation of the garage into a workspace.

Ein anregendes Umfeld ist in der Lage, die Kreativität zu fördern. Das war wohl der Gedanke des Inhabers dieser ehemaligen Garage, als er sie seiner Tochter, einer Architekturstudentin, überließ. Ein einzigartiges einzelnes Möbelstück steht im Mittelpunkt der Umwandlung dieser Garage in einen Arbeitsbereich.

Il s'agit d'un environnement stimulant la créativité. C'est ce qu'a sans doute imaginé l'ancien propriétaire de ce garage lorsqu'il l'a donné à sa fille, étudiante en architecture. Un élément unique du mobilier est l'acteur de la transformation du garage en un espace de travail.

Un entorno estimulante es capaz de promover la creatividad. Es lo que debió pensar el propietario de este antiguo garaje cuando se lo dio a su hija, una estudiante de arquitectura. Una única pieza de mobiliario es el foco de la transformación del garaje en un espacio de trabajo.

www.ruetemple.ru // Team: Alexander Kudimov and Daria Butakhina

During demolition, the dropped ceiling was removed to unexpectedly reveal a system of roof trusses worth incorporating into the design of the new workshop. Three types of wood were used for flooring, wall panelling and furniture.

Beim Abriss wurde die Zwischendecke entfernt, wodurch unerwartet ein System von Dachsparren freigelegt wurde, das sich lohnte, in die Gestaltung der neuen Werkstatt eingebunden zu werden. Für Bodenbelag, Wandverkleidung und Möbel wurden drei Holzarten verwendet.

Pendant les travaux, le faux plafond a été enlevé, ce qui a révélé un système de fermettes inattendu qui méritait d'être incorporé à la conception du nouvel atelier. Trois types de bois différents ont été utilisés pour le sol, l'habillage des murs et le mobilier.

En la demolición, se eliminó el falso techo y sorprendentemente quedó al descubierto un sistema de cerchas que merece la pena incorporar en el diseño del nuevo taller. Se utilizaron tres tipos de madera para el solado, el revestimiento de paredes y los muebles.

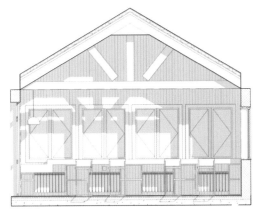

Section 1

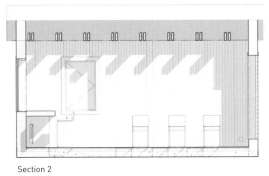
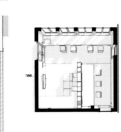

Section 2

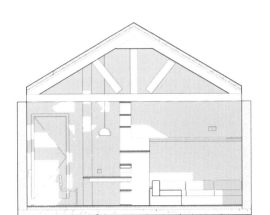

Section 3

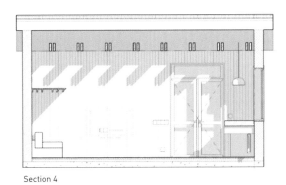

Section 4

Section 5

Section 6

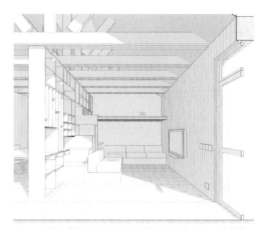

Perspective view 1

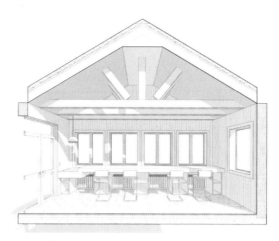

Perspective view 2

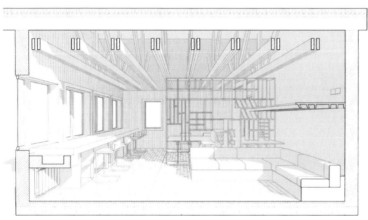

Perspective view 3

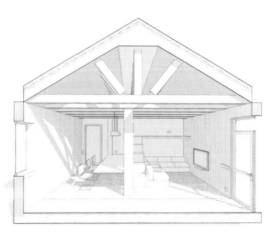

Perspective view 4

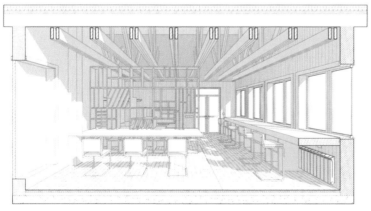

Perspective view 5

Axonometric view

A single piece of furniture generates various areas for different functions, integrating plenty of shelving, a desk, a sofa, and even a loft bed. The shelving system is open, maintaining the open character of the space.

Ein einziges Möbelstück schafft verschiedene Bereiche für unterschiedliche Funktionen und integriert eine Vielzahl von Regalen, einen Schreibtisch, ein Sofa und sogar ein Hochbett. Das Regalsystem ist offen und bewahrt so den offenen Charakter des Raumes.

Un seul meuble, comprenant un bon nombre d'étagères, un bureau, un canapé, et même un lit en mezzanine, permet de diviser le lieu en plusieurs espaces de fonctions différentes. Le système de rayonnage accentue ici le caractère décloisonné de la pièce.

Una única pieza de mobiliario da lugar a varias zonas para diferentes funciones, con muchas estanterías, un escritorio, un sofá e incluso, una cama en altura. El sistema de estanterías está abierto, manteniendo así el carácter abierto del espacio.

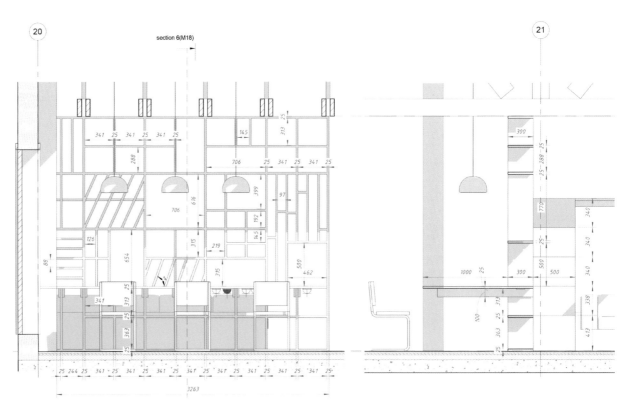

Section 7

Section 8

The piece of furniture is an open shelving system for easy access from two sides. Further, it doesn't block views, maintaining the open character of the original space.

Das Möbelstück ist ein offenes Regalsystem, das von zwei Seiten bequem zugänglich ist. Zudem versperrt es nicht den Ausblick und bewahrt so den offenen Charakter des ursprünglichen Raumes.

Le meuble est un système de rayonnage ouvert accessible des deux côtés. Le fait qu'il n'obstrue pas la vue accentue le caractère ouvert de l'espace d'origine.

Las estanterías son abiertas en los dos lados para un fácil acceso. Además, no bloquea las vistas, manteniendo el carácter abierto del espacio original.

This striking space, functional and comfortable at the same time, was mainly designed as a workplace, but can easily be used as a living quarter with a loft bed included.

Dieser bemerkenswerte Raum, der gleichzeitig funktionell und komfortabel ist, war vor allem als Arbeitsplatz konzipiert, kann jedoch leicht als Wohnbereich mit Hochbett genutzt werden.

Cet espace étonnant, à la fois fonctionnel et confortable, a été principalement conçu comme un lieu de travail, mais peut facilement être utilisé comme pièce de vie en y incluant un lit en mezzanine.

Este espacio tan llamativo como funcional y cómodo, se diseñó principalmente como un lugar de trabajo, pudiendo ser fácilmente utilizado como salón que incluye una cama en alto.

PENTHOUSE V // BEEF ARCHITEKTI

BRATISLAVA, SLOVAKIA

With unusual forms and an unconventional space organization, the design of this penthouse is inspired by the natural world. Bespoke pieces of cabinetry, such as the floor-to-ceiling wall unit in the kitchen, the wardrobe in the bedroom, and the floating sideboard in the dining area provide specific storage for each of the areas.

Mit den ungewöhnlichen Formen und einer unkonventionellen Raumaufteilung ist die Gestaltung dieses Penthouse von der Welt der Natur inspiriert. Individuell angefertigte Schränke wie die raumhohe Wandeinheit in der Küche, der Kleiderschrank im Schlafzimmer und das schwebende Sideboard im Essbereich bieten einen spezifischen Stauraum für den jeweiligen Bereich.

Avec ses formes inhabituelles et son organisation de l'espace atypique, l'architecture intérieure de ce penthouse s'inspire de la nature. Des meubles d'ébénistes réalisés sur mesure, tels que le meuble de cuisine équipée, l'armoire de la chambre et le buffet flottant dans le coin-repas offrent des solutions de rangement spécifique pour chacun des espaces.

Con formas inusuales y una organización del espacio poco convencional, el diseño de este ático se inspira en el mundo natural. Piezas de ebanistería realizadas a medida, como el armario del suelo al techo de la cocina, el armario en el dormitorio y el aparador flotante en la zona comedor proporcionan espacio de almacenaje específico en estas áreas.

www.beef.sk // Team: Radoslav Buzinkay, Andrej FerenĐík, and Jakub ViskupiĐ

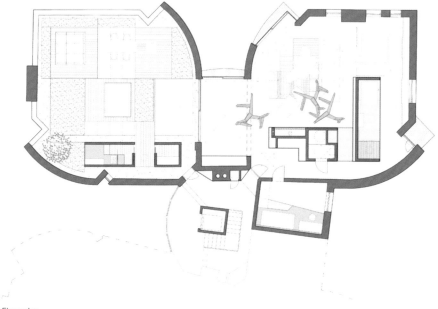

Floor plan

Metal sheet fins stick out from a wooden wall to provide shelving space with a sculptural quality. The shelves are close together, rather than the typical average spacing of 30 centimetres between shelves.

Metallblechflossen ragen aus einer Holzwand heraus und sorgen für Regalraum mit plastischer Qualität. Die Regale sind dicht beieinander, anstatt den typischen Durchschnittsabstand von 30 Zentimetern zwischen den Regalen einzuhalten.

Des ailerons de métal ressortent d'un mur en bois pour offrir un rayonnage aux qualités sculpturales. Les étagères sont assez rapprochées plutôt qu'espacées de 30 centimètres en moyenne.

Las láminas de metal sobresalen de la pared de madera para proporcionar un espacio de almacenaje de gran calidad escultural. Las estanterías están muy próximas entre sí, lejos de la medida estándar de 30 centímetros entre estantes.

The kitchen's storage cabinets and appliances are concealed behind floor-to-ceiling wood pivoting pocket doors. This system offers the advantage of keeping the cabinets in an open position with no door in the way.

Die Küchenschränke und -geräte sind hinter raumhohen schwenkbaren Taschenschiebetüren aus Holz verborgen. Dieses System bietet den Vorteil, dass die Schränke geöffnet bleiben können, ohne dass eine Tür im Weg ist.

Les placards et appareils de la cuisine sont dissimulés derrière des panneaux escamotables en bois pouvant pivoter intégralement. Ce système offre l'avantage de pouvoir ouvrir les placards sans être gêné par des portes.

Los armarios de la cocina y los electrodomésticos se ocultan tras unas puertas pivotantes de madera del suelo al techo. Este sistema ofrece la ventaja de mantener los armarios abiertos sin puertas entremedias.

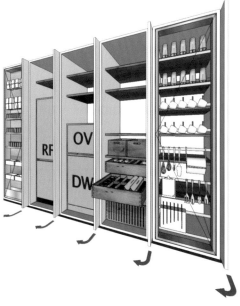

Perspective view of kitchen wall unit

In keeping with the natural and rustic design aesthetic of the penthouse, the front of the bedroom's closet is made of multiple sliding doors. The slatted design camouflages the edges of the doors, achieving a seamless look.

Im Einklang mit der natürlichen und rustikalen Design-Ästhetik des Penthouse besteht die Frontseite des Wandschranks im Schlafzimmer aus mehreren Schiebetüren. Das Lattendesign tarnt die Ränder der Türen und schafft dadurch eine nahtlose Optik.

En harmonie avec l'esthétique naturelle et rustique du penthouse, le devant du placard de la chambre est composé de multiples portes coulissantes. Le design en forme de lattes en fait disparaître les arêtes et lui donne un aspect lisse.

En consonancia con la estética natural y rústica del diseño de este ático, el frontal del armario del dormitorio consiste en varias puertas correderas. El diseño en listones camufla las terminaciones de las puertas, de forma que el frontal parece ser una única pieza.

STEEL STOOL // NOON STUDIO

www.noon-studio.com

When it comes to space saving, nothing is more efficient than a multifunctional piece of furniture. The no-screw, no-glue stool can be used as a side table or as a magazine rack. Stack a few together and you get a modular shelving system. The precision of assembly allows the stool to hold its components perfectly tight in place.

Wenn es darum geht, Platz zu sparen, ist nichts effizienter als ein Multifunktionsmöbelstück. Der Hocker ohne Schrauben und ohne Leim kann als Beistelltisch oder Zeitschriftenhalter eingesetzt werden. Stapeln Sie einige davon übereinander - und Sie erhalten ein modulares Regalsystem. Die Präzision der Montage lässt den Schemel seine Komponenten perfekt an der richtigen Stelle halten.

Pour ce qui est d'économiser l'espace, rien n'est plus efficace qu'un meuble multifonctionnel. Ce tabouret sans vis ni colle peut servir de table de chevet ou de porte-revues. En l'empilant sur d'autres, on obtient un système d'étagères modulable. La précision de l'assemblage lui permet de maintenir ses composantes bien fermement en place.

Cuando se trata de ahorrar espacio, un mueble multifuncional resulta la mejor opción. El taburete realizado sin tornillos ni pegamento puede utilizarse como mesa auxiliar o como estante para revistas. Se pueden apilar unos cuantos y obtener así un sistema de estanterías modulares. La precisión del montaje permite que el taburete mantenga sus componentes perfectamente ajustados en su lugar.

Manufacturer: Noon Studio // Team: Gautier Pelegrin and Vincent Taïani
Materials: Black epoxy powder-coated 2 mm thick steel sheet, oiled ash wood

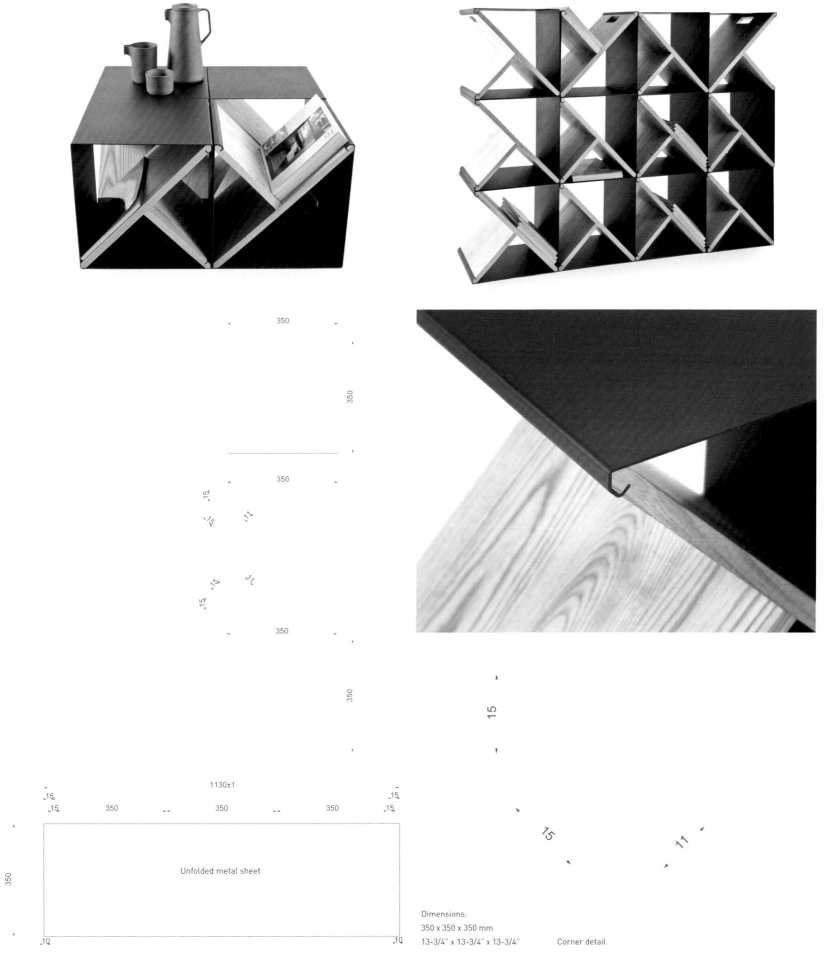

350

350

350

350

350

.15 .11

.15 .11

.15 .11

15

15

11

1130±1

.15 .15

.15 350 350 350 .15

350

Unfolded metal sheet

.10 .10

Dimensions:
350 x 350 x 350 mm
13-3/4" x 13-3/4" x 13-3/4"   Corner detail

100 m² // 1,076sq ft

STABLE IN WEST FLANDERS // STUDIO FARRIS ARCHITECTS

WEST FLANDERS, BELGIUM

The owner of a farm with several buildings wanted to have a small office so he would be able to work from home at times. The stable, no longer in use, was gutted. Only the shell of the building was maintained. This original structure then became the container of a new structure.

Der Besitzer eines Bauernhofes mit mehreren Gebäuden wollte ein kleines Büro haben, damit er manchmal von Zuhause aus arbeiten kann. Hierfür wurde der Stall, der nicht mehr in Gebrauch ist, entkernt und nur das Rohbauskelett des Gebäudes beibehalten. Diese ursprüngliche Bausubstanz wurde das Behältnis eines neuen Gebäudes.

Le propriétaire d'une ferme comprenant plusieurs bâtiments voulait un petit bureau pour pouvoir parfois travailler depuis chez lui. L'écurie, inoccupée, a été totalement vidée. Seule la structure extérieure du bâtiment a été préservée. Cette structure a accueilli une nouvelle architecture en son sein.

El propietario de una granja con varias construcciones quería tener una pequeña oficina que le permitiera trabajar a veces desde casa. El establo, ya sin uso, fue destruido. Solo se mantuvo el armazón del edificio. Esta original estructura se convirtió así en el contenedor de una estructura nueva.

www.studiofarris.com // Giuseppe Farris

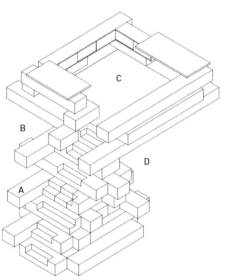

Axonometric view of the new wood
structure

A. Reading area
B. Library
C. Workspace
D. Meeting room

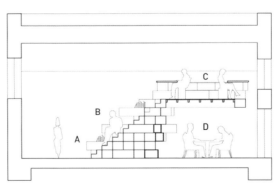

Longitudinal section

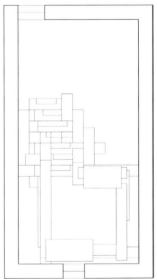

Plan view

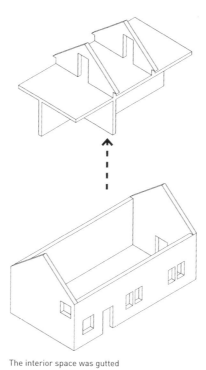

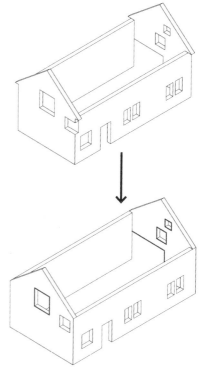

Original building

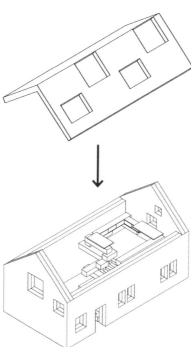

The interior space was gutted

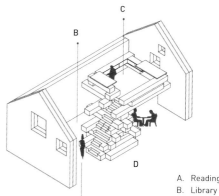

New windows were added and a new 'concrete box' was inserted into the original volume.

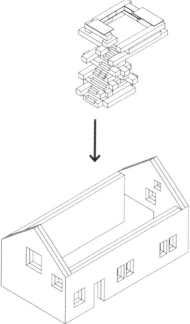

Avoiding the creation of a new intermediary floor, a freestanding wood structure was inserted inside the existing building

The new roof has various skylights

C
B
D
A

A. Reading area
B. Library
C. Office
D. Meeting room

The architect designed a freestanding large piece of furniture that divides the space into different areas to maintain the open character of the space.

Der Architekt entwarf ein freistehendes großes Möbelstück, das den Raum in unterschiedliche Bereiche aufteilt, um den offenen Charakter des Raumes zu bewahren.

L'architecte a conçu un grand meuble autonome qui divise l'espace en différentes zones et laisse de grands espaces de circulation.

El arquitecto diseñó un gran mueble independiente que divide el espacio en diferentes áreas y así mantiene el carácter abierto del mismo.

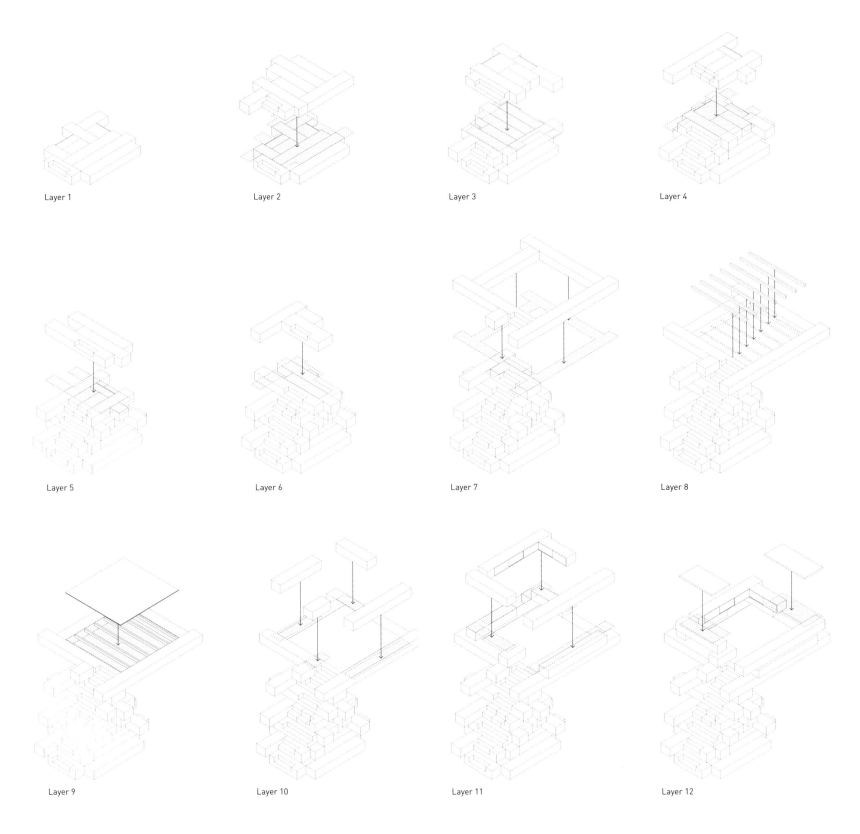

Layer 1

Layer 2

Layer 3

Layer 4

Layer 5

Layer 6

Layer 7

Layer 8

Layer 9

Layer 10

Layer 11

Layer 12

This piece of furniture is made out of timber beams stacked following an orthogonal grid to form bookshelves and provide for seating. The configuration of the stacked beams also creates a stair that leads to a workspace on the second level.

Dieses Möbelstück besteht aus Holzbalken, die zu einem rechtwinkligen Gitter gestapelt werden, das Bücherregale bildet und für Sitzgelegenheiten sorgt. Die Anordnung der gestapelten Balken bildet auch eine Treppe, die zu einem Arbeitsbereich auf der zweiten Ebene führt.

Ce meuble est fait de poutres de bois empilées selon une grille orthogonale pour obtenir des étagères et de quoi s'asseoir. La configuration de ces poutres crée également un escalier qui mène à un espace bureau au deuxième niveau.

Este mueble está hecho de vigas de madera apiladas que siguen una cuadrícula ortogonal que forma estanterías y lugares para sentarse. La configuración de las vigas apiladas crea también una escalera que conduce a un espacio de trabajo en el segundo piso.

The office space includes a meeting room, a library, office desks and a reading nook that doubles as resting area.

Die Bürofläche umfasst auch einen Konferenzraum, eine Bibliothek, Büroschreibtische und eine Leseecke, die auch als Ruhebereich dient.

L'espace bureau comprend une salle de réunion, une bibliothèque, des bureaux et un coin lecture qui peut servir de coin repos.

El espacio de oficina incluye una sala de reuniones, una biblioteca, escritorios de oficina y un rincón de lectura que se duplica y convierte en zona de descanso.

79 m² // 850 sq ft

Photo © Asen Emilov

APARTMENT V01 // DONTDIY

SOFIA, BULGARIA

Maximizing natural lighting and creating a comfortable living environment were the primary goals in the redesign of this apartment. The vestibule was enlarged at the expense of a utilities room, and the existing kitchen was transformed into a dressing room. The storage requirement was satisfied by both built-ins and freestanding units.

Die natürliche Beleuchtung zu maximieren und einen komfortablen Wohnraum zu schaffen, waren die vorrangingen Ziele bei der Neugestaltung dieser Wohnung. Die Diele wurde auf Kosten des Hauswirtschaftsraums vergrößert, und die bestehende Küche wurde in ein Ankleidezimmer umgewandelt. Sowohl Einbauten als auch freistehende Elemente erfüllen den Bedarf an Stauraum.

Cet appartement a été réaménagé pour créer un intérieur confortable tout en utilisant la lumière naturelle de manière optimale. Le vestibule a été agrandi aux dépens de la buanderie et la cuisine d'origine a été transformée en dressing. Les exigences en matière de rangement ont été satisfaites aussi bien par des modules encastrés que par des modules autonomes.

Los principales objetivos en el rediseño de este apartamento fueron la maximización de la luz natural y la creación de un ambiente confortable para la vida en él. El vestíbulo se amplió para crear un lavadero y la cocina existente se transformó en un vestidor. El requisito de almacenamiento fue satisfecho con la creación de piezas integradas e independientes.

www.dontdiy.org // Team: dontDIY

The fireplace is integrated into a full height wall cabinet, which also contains the refrigerator and the air-conditioning unit. Painted white to match the walls, it contributes to the creation of an unencumbered layout.

Ein Wandschrank in voller Höhe beherbergt Kamin, Kühlschrank und Klimaanlage. Passend zu den Wänden Weiß gestrichen, trägt er zur Schaffung einer unbelasteten Gestaltung bei.

La cheminée est intégrée dans une armoire murale qui renferme également le réfrigérateur et le climatiseur. Peinte en blanc pour être assortie aux murs, elle contribue à l'aménagement d'un espace aéré.

La chimenea se integra en un armario con altura de suelo a techo, que también contiene el frigorífico y el aire acondicionado. Pintado de color blanco para que coincida con las paredes, contribuye a crear una sensación de amplitud.

The new kitchen, made of plywood built-ins, is attuned to the bookcase in the living area. When not in use, it can disappear behind sliding panels, adding to the clean look of the apartment.

Die neue Küche, die aus Sperrholzeinbauten besteht, ist auf das Bücherregal im Wohnbereich abgestimmt. Wird sie gerade nicht genutzt, kann sie hinter Schiebepaneelen verschwinden und verleiht der Wohnung eine saubere Optik.

La nouvelle cuisine, constituée de modules encastrés en contreplaqué, s'harmonise avec la bibliothèque du séjour. Quand elle n'est pas utilisée, elle peut disparaître derrière des panneaux coulissants, ce qui accentue l'aspect épuré de cet appartement.

La nueva cocina, empotrada y realizada en madera contrachapada, está en sintonía con la librería del salón. Cuando no se usa, desaparece detrás de los paneles deslizantes, lo que da lugar a que haya una vista limpia del apartamento.

223

A brightly coloured freestanding bookshelf is made to stand out, as opposed to a wall of integrated cabinets with their fronts finished in the same colour as the walls around them to make them disappear.

Ein freistehendes knallbuntes Bücherregal soll alle Blicke auf sich ziehen.- Dies steht im Kontrast zu einer Wand aus integrierten Schränken, deren Frontseiten in der gleichen Farbe wie die Wände um sie herum verarbeitet sind, um sie verschwinden zu lassen.

Une bibliothèque aux couleurs vives s'oppose à un mur aux nombreux placards encastrés dont la couleur se confond avec celle des autres murs de la pièce.

Destaca una librería independiente de colores brillantes, en contraposición con la pared de armarios integrados con sus frentes terminados en el mismo color que las paredes de su alrededor para camuflarlos.

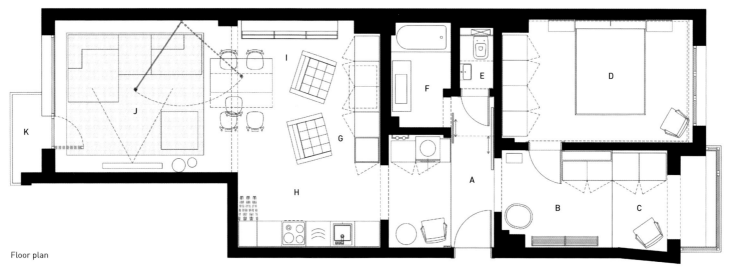

Floor plan

A. Vestibule
B. Boudoir
C. Yoga/deck
D. Bedroom
E. Toilet room
F. Bathroom

G. Seating area
H. Concealed kitchen
I. Workspace/
    dining area
J. TV area
K. Balcony

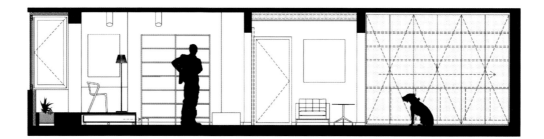

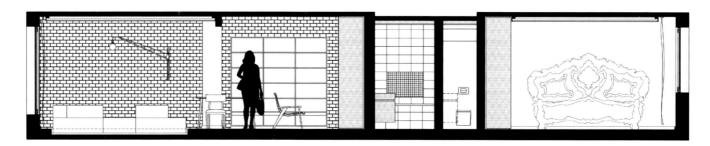

Sections

Both the bedroom and the bathroom are minimal, sparsely furnished and equipped with just what is essential.

Sowohl Schlafzimmer als auch Bad sind minimal, spärlich eingerichtet und nur mit dem Wichtigsten ausgestattet.

L'aménagement de la chambre et de la salle de bains est minimaliste. Les pièces sont peu meublées et équipées uniquement de l'essentiel.

Tanto el dormitorio como el baño son minimalistas, escasamente amueblados y equipados con lo esencial.

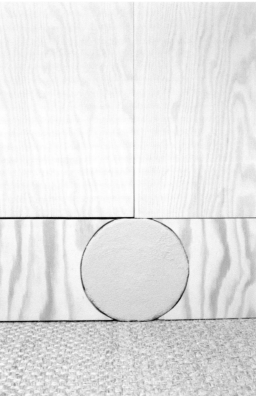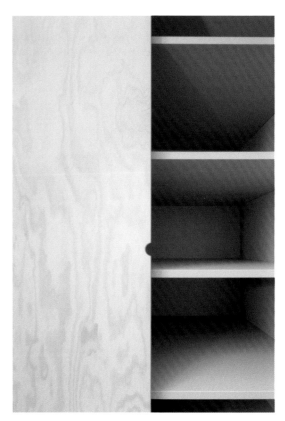

56 m² // 603 sq ft

Photo © Yann Laubscher

INHABITED WOODEN WALLS // AURÉLIE MONET KASISI
GENEVA, SWITZERLAND

The owners of a family house wanted to create storage in two large rooms and divide each into two smaller ones to accommodate different household programs. Two structures —one for each room— provide abundant storage and partitions off the rooms to create a home cinema, a playroom, a small office and a bedroom for an au pair.

Die Besitzer dieses Familienhauses wollten in zwei großen Räumen Stauraum schaffen und diese jeweils in zwei kleinere unterteilen, um verschiedene Haushaltsfunktionen darin unterzubringen. Zwei Strukturen - jeweils eine pro Raum - sorgen für reichlich Stauraum und Trennwände außerhalb der Räume, um ein Heimkino, ein Spielzimmer, ein kleines Büro sowie ein Schlafzimmer für ein Au-pair zu schaffen.

Les propriétaires de cette maison familiale voulaient créer du rangement dans deux grandes pièces et diviser chacune d'elles en deux plus petites pour accueillir des usages domestiques différents. Deux structures – une par pièce – offrent de nombreux rangements et les cloisons issues de ces pièces accueillent un home cinéma, une salle de jeux, un petit bureau et une chambre pour une jeune fille au pair.

Los propietarios de esta residencia familiar querían dividir dos grandes estancias para crear habitaciones más pequeñas destinadas a distintas funciones y, a la vez, conseguir más espacio de almacenaje. Se usaron sendas estructuras que proporcionan lugares de gran almacenaje y dividen las estancias, creando así un espacio independiente para un cine en casa, una sala de juegos, una pequeña oficina y un dormitorio para la *au pair*.

www.monetkasisi.ch // Team: Aurélie Monet Kasisi
Carpenter: Fabien Pont

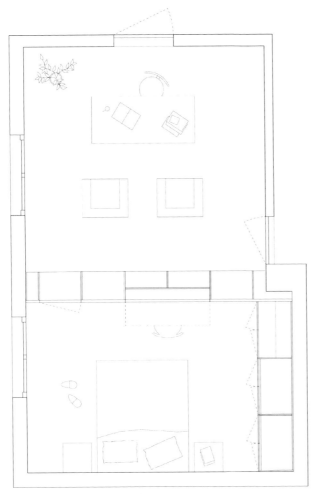

Office and au pair bedroom floor plan

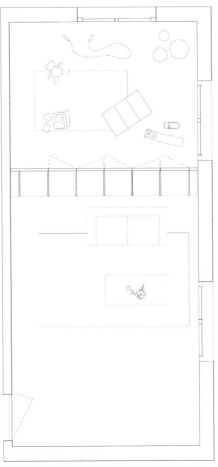

Home cinema and playroom floor plan

One of the bookshelf stores the family's large CD collection and a beamer for the home cinema. Behind the bookshelf is the playroom with a circular opening that adds a playful accent to the structure, while allowing parents to keep an eye on their kids.

Eines der Bücherregale beherbergt die große CD-Sammlung der Familie und einen Beamer für das Heimkino. Hinter dem Bücherregal ist das Spielzimmer mit einer kreisförmigen Öffnung, die der Struktur einen spielerischen Akzent verleiht und es den Eltern gleichzeitig ermöglicht, ein Auge auf ihre Kinder zu haben.

L'une des étagères permet de ranger l'immense collection de CD de la famille et le Beamer du home-cinéma. Derrière l'étagère se trouve la salle de jeux dont l'ouverture circulaire renforce l'accent ludique de la structure, tout en permettant aux parents de garder un œil sur leurs enfants.

Una de las librerías permite almacenar la gran colección de CDs de la familia y un proyector para disfrutar del cine en casa. Detrás está la zona de juegos con una abertura circular que le da un carácter divertido a la estructura y permite que los padres no pierden de vista a los niños.

A series of small accessories, including a movable wooden stepped block in the play-room, storage boxes and nightstands were also designed to complete the furnishing of the new rooms.

Eine Reihe kleiner Zusatzgeräte, darunter ein beweglicher Holzstufenblock im Spielzimmer, Aufbewahrungsbehälter und Nachttische wurden so gestaltet, dass sie die Ausstattung der neuen Räume vervollständigen.

Une série de petits accessoires, notamment le bloc de bois mobile dans la salle de jeux, les boîtes de rangement et les lampes de chevet ont également été conçus pour parfaire le mobilier des nouvelles chambres.

Se diseñaron una serie de pequeños accesorios para completar el mobiliario de las nuevas habitaciones, como un bloque de madera con escalones en la sala de juegos, cajas de almacenaje y mesitas.

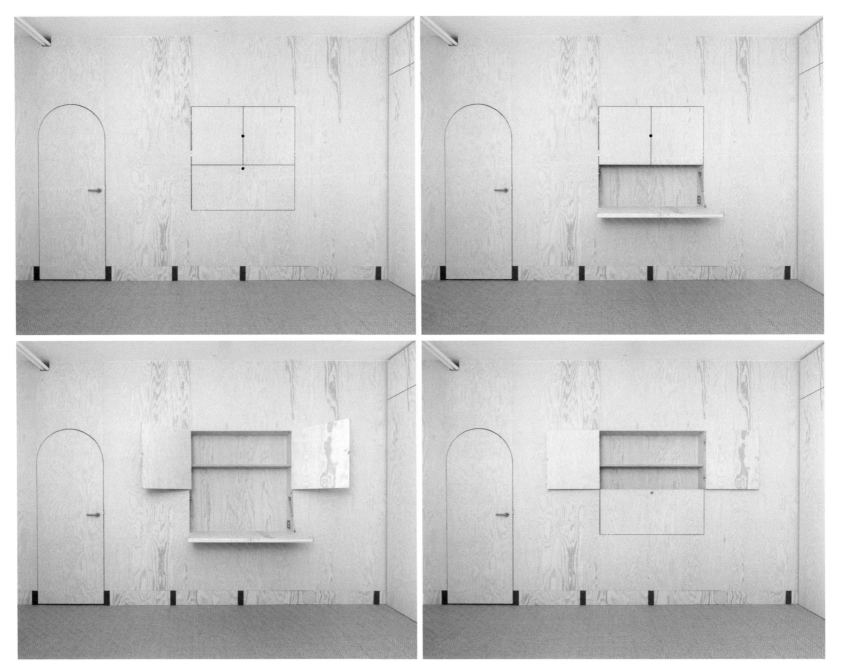

The other bookshelf provides the office with plenty of shelving space. A door gives access to a bedroom on the other side of the bookshelf. The bedroom has a closet with brightly painted interior and a fold-way desk.

Das andere Bücherregal schenkt dem Büro reichlich Ablageflächen. Eine Tür ermöglicht den Zugang zu einem Schlafzimmer auf der anderen Seite des Bücherregals. Das Schlafzimmer hat einen Wandschrank, der innen in hellen Farben gestrichen ist, sowie einen faltbaren Schreibtisch.

La seconde tablette sert de bureau et dispose d'un espace considérable pour placer des étagères. La porte permet d'accéder à la chambre située de l'autre côté de la bibliothèque. Dans cette chambre, l'intérieur du placard est peint de couleurs vives. Elle dispose aussi d'un bureau rabattable.

La otra librería dispone de muchas estanterías para la oficina. Incluye una puerta que da acceso al dormitorio. El dormitorio tiene un armario cuyo interior está pintado en tonos vivos e incluye un escritorio plegable.

The bookshelves are made of oiled pine. They sit on colourful feet made of recycled bricks and landscape edging elements either protruding from underneath the bookshelves or flush with the face of the piece of furniture.

Die Bücherregale bestehen aus geölter Kiefer. Sie sitzen auf bunten Füßen aus aufbereiteten Ziegelsteinen und Elementen, die die Umgebung begrenzen. Sie treten entweder unter den Bücherregalen hervor oder schließen bündig mit der Frontseite des Möbelstücks ab.

La bibliothèque est en pin verni. Elle repose sur des pieds colorés faits de briques recyclées et d'éléments de bordure de jardin qui font saillie sous les étagères ou sont alignés sur le devant du meuble.

Las estanterías están realizadas en pino tratado con aceite. Se asientan en pies muy coloridos, realizados con ladrillos reciclados y adoquines del jardín que sobresalen o se alinean con el frontal del mueble.

Photo © Natalia Geci

LYNKO NOMADIC FURNITURE SYSTEM // NATALIA GECI

www.nataliageci.com

LINKO is a freestanding modular system, completely customisable. Different sized metal frames and wooden hinges allow for an innumerable amount of configurations alongside different accessories such as mirrors, hooks, hangers, trays, shelves, and storage pockets.

LINKO ist ein freistehendes, komplett anpassbares Modulsystem. Metallrahmen in verschiedenen Größen und Holzscharniere ermöglichen neben unterschiedlichem Zubehör wie Spiegeln, Haken, Kleiderbügeln, Behältern, Regalen und Aufbewahrungstaschen eine endlose Anzahl von Konfigurationen.

LINKO est un système modulaire autoportant, entièrement personnalisable. Une quantité innombrable de configurations différentes voient le jour en agençant des cadres en métal et des charnières en bois de différentes tailles, ainsi que des accessoires tels que les miroirs, crochets, cintres, plateaux, étagères et sacs de rangement.

LINKO es un sistema modular independiente, completamente personalizable. Diferentes tamaños de marcos de metal y bisagras de madera permiten innumerables configuraciones con accesorios como espejos, ganchos, perchas, bandejas, estantes y organizadores con bolsillos.

LINKO was the winner of a Platinum A' Design Award, 2016-2017. Production upon request through designer.
Materials: Copper, chrome, white, red, orange, and bronze frames; chinaberry and oak hinges; cowhide, fabric, and felt.

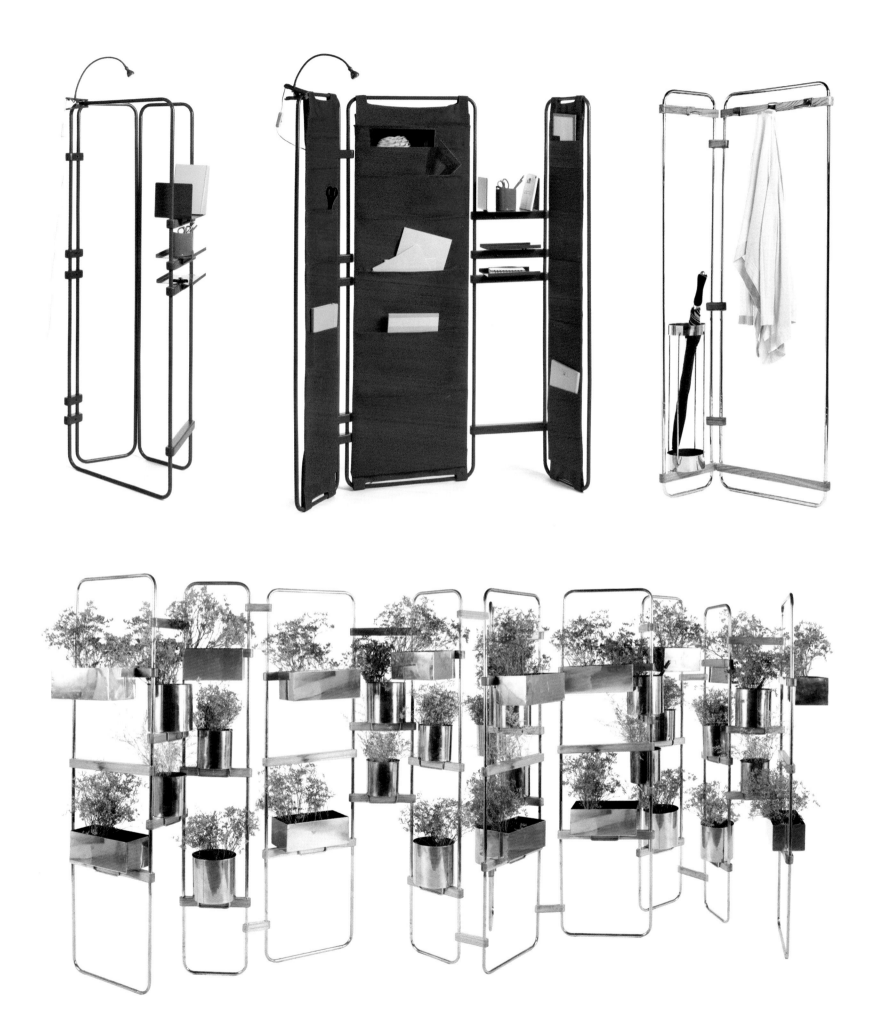

PLAY

WASH

TRAVEL

EAT

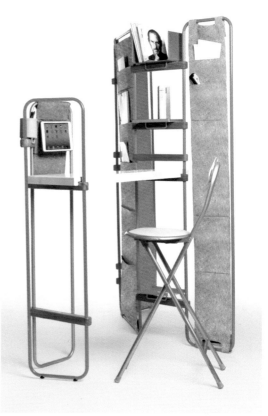

WORK

DRESS

RELAX

The frames can be moved by the hinges to adapt to any space. They can also be folded flat for storage or easy transportation when needed. More frames and hinges, as well as accessories, can be added to the structure at any time.

Die Rahmen können durch Scharniere so bewegt werden, dass sie sich an jeden Raum anpassen. Zum Aufbewahren oder für einen einfachen Transport können sie bei Bedarf auch flach zusammengefaltet werden. Die Struktur kann jederzeit durch weitere Rahmen und Scharniere sowie Zubehör ergänzt werden.

Les cadres peuvent être manipulés au niveau des charnières pour s'adapter à toute configuration d'espace. Ils peuvent également être rabattus à plat pour faciliter le rangement ou le transport en cas de besoin. À tout moment, il est possible d'ajouter des cadres et des charnières, ainsi que des accessoires à la structure.

Los marcos se pueden mover con las bisagras para adaptarse a cualquier espacio. También se pueden plegar para guardarlos o transportarlos cuando sea necesario. A la estructura se le pueden añadir, en cualquier momento, marcos y bisagras, al igual que accesorios.

- 5 mm thick mirror
- Metal sheet base,
  1.6 mm thick with
  rotating tube
- Metal frame
- Copper plating finish

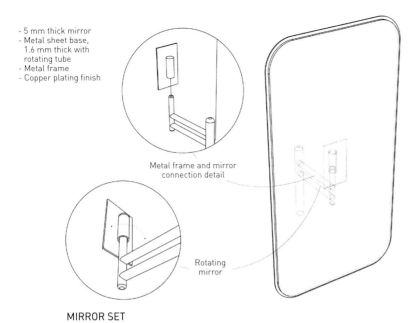

Metal frame and mirror
connection detail

Rotating
mirror

MIRROR SET

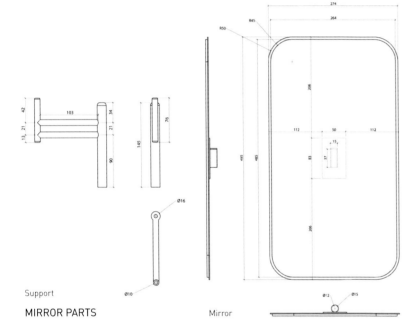

Support

MIRROR PARTS

Mirror

- Top metal sheet, 1.6 mm thick
- Bottom metal sheet, 2 mm thick
- Gripping rods, 4 mm diameter
- Copper plating finish

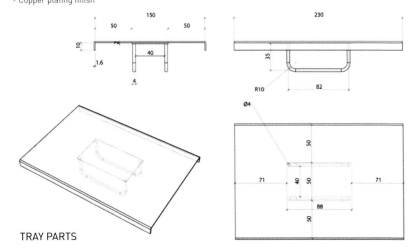

TRAY PARTS

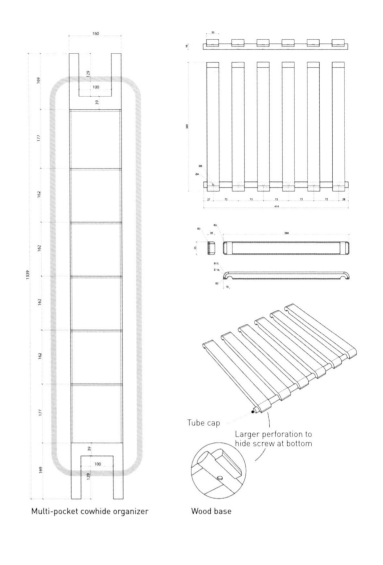

Multi-pocket cowhide organizer

Wood base

Tube cap

Larger perforation to
hide screw at bottom

- Tube 5/8'' diameter,
  1.6 mm thick

Metal frames

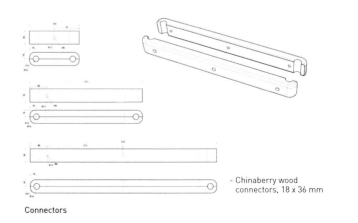

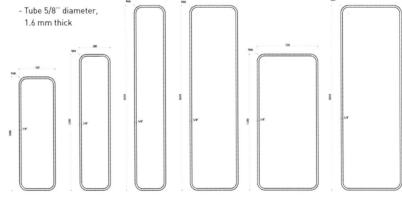

Connectors

- Chinaberry wood
  connectors, 18 x 36 mm

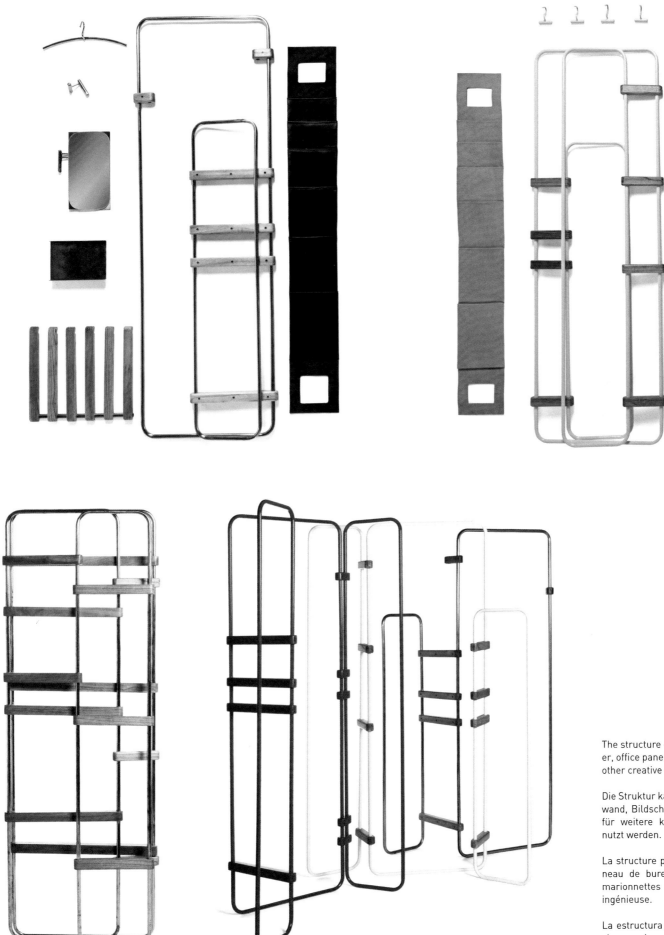

The structure can be used as clothes hanger, office panel, screen, puppet theatre, and other creative configurations.

Die Struktur kann als Kleiderständer, Stellwand, Bildschirm, Marionettentheater und für weitere kreative Konfigurationen benutzt werden.

La structure peut servir de cintre, de panneau de bureau, d'écran, de théâtre de marionnettes ou toute autre configuration ingénieuse.

La estructura se puede utilizar como percha para la ropa, tablero de oficina, biombo, teatro de títeres y para otras originales configuraciones.

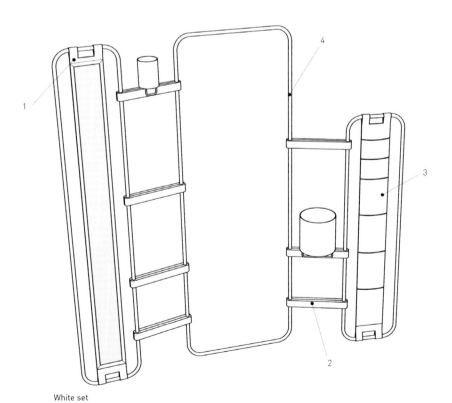

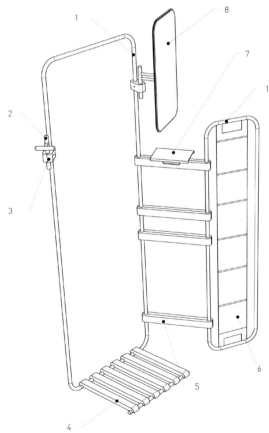

White set

1. Mirror with cowhide straps
2. Connectors in Chinaberry wood
3. Multi-pocket cowhide organizer
4. Frames and accessories
   finished in white

Set option

1. Metal frame	5. Large connector
2. Coat hook	6. Multi-pocket
3. Small connector	cowhide organizer
4. Metal and wood	7. Tray
base	8. Mirror

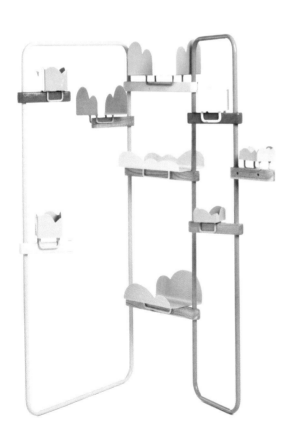

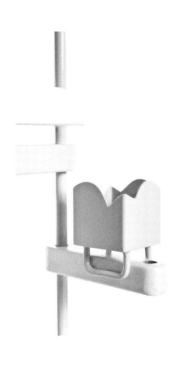

141 m² // 1,518 sq ft

TERRACED HOUSE // MILI MŁODZI LUDZIE

POZNAŃ, POLAND

Most of the materials found during the remodel of this house were in good condition. This encouraged the idea of preserving as many elements of the house as possible, including the wood staircase, doors, wood flooring, and the fireplace. These existing elements were treated as the base for the design of the main storage solutions.

Das meiste Material, das während der Umgestaltung dieses Hauses auftauchte, war in gutem Zustand. Diese Tatsache ermutigte die Planer, so viele Elemente des Hauses wie möglich zu erhalten, darunter die Holztreppe, die Türen, den Holzboden und den Kamin. Diese vorhandenen Elemente wurden als Grundlage für die Gestaltung der wichtigsten Stauraumlösungen berücksichtigt.

La plupart des matériaux trouvés au cours du remaniement de cette maison étaient en bon état, encourageant l'idée de conserver autant d'éléments de la maison que possible, y compris l'escalier en bois, les portes, le plancher et la cheminée. Ces éléments d'origine ont servi de base pour concevoir les principales solutions de rangement.

La mayoría de los materiales que se encontraron durante la remodelación de esta casa estaban en buenas condiciones. Esto animó la idea de preservar todos los elementos de la casa que fuera posible, incluyendo la escalera de madera, las puertas, el suelo de madera y la chimenea. Los elementos ya existentes sirvieron de base para el diseño de las principales soluciones de almacenamiento.

www.milimlodziludzie.com // Team: Przemysław Nowak, and Lech Moczulski

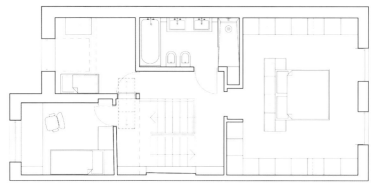

First floor plan

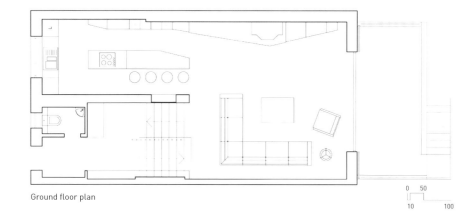

Ground floor plan

0   50

10   100

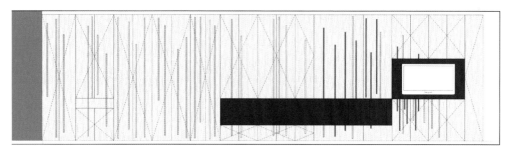

Cabinet unit front elevation

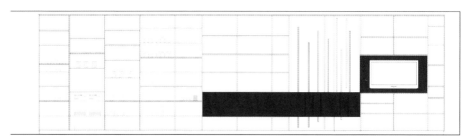

Cabinet unit interior elevation

Cabinet unit plan

The client requested an open kitchen as part of a spacious living area; a place where the cook could interact with family members and friends. A continuous undulating wall unit integrating the refurbished fireplace emphasises the connection between the kitchen and the living area. On the opposite wall, a new wine bottle rack acts as a counterpoint.

Der Kunde verlangte eine offene Küche als Teil eines geräumigen Wohnbereichs; ein Ort, an dem der Koch mit Familienmitgliedern und Freunden interagieren kann. Eine durchgehende wellenförmige Wandeinheit, die den renovierten Kamin integriert, unterstreicht die Verbindung zwischen Küche und Wohnbereich. An der gegenüberliegenden Wand dient ein neues Weinregal als Kontrapunkt.

Le client désirait une cuisine ouverte dans une spacieuse pièce à vivre, un endroit où il serait possible de cuisiner tout en interagissant avec des membres de la famille et des amis. Un mur continu ondoyant intégrant la cheminée rénovée accentue la connexion entre la cuisine et le salon. Sur le mur opposé, un nouveau casier à bouteilles lui sert de contrepoint.

El cliente solicitó una cocina abierta que formase parte de una zona de estar amplia, un lugar donde el cocinero pudiese interactuar con los familiares y amigos. Un armario de pared, ondulado y continuo que integra la chimenea remodelada enfatiza la conexión entre la cocina y la zona de estar. En la pared opuesta, un nuevo botellero actúa como contrapunto.

The custom designed bookshelf on the first floor landing harmonises with the pre-existing staircase guardrail, contributing to a unified design aesthetic throughout the house.

Das individuell gestaltete Bücherregal am Treppenabsatz des ersten Stockwerks harmonisiert mit dem Handlauf der bereits bestehenden Treppe und trägt zu einer einheitlichen Designästhetik im ganzen Haus bei.

Cette étagère conçue spécialement pour le premier étage s'harmonise avec le garde-corps d'origine de l'escalier, ce qui donne une impression d'unité à l'esthétique générale de toute la maison.

En el primer piso, en el rellano de la escalera, la librería a medida armoniza con la barandilla ya existente, contribuyendo a unificar la estética del diseño en toda la casa.

Rather than going for an off-the-shelf wardrobe in the nursery, the design team proposed a much more space efficient and creative storage solution consisting of a large pullout cabinet that slides along tracks attached to the ceiling.

Anstatt sich für einen handelsüblichen Kleiderschrank im Kinderzimmer zu entscheiden, schlug das Designteam eine deutlich kreativere Stauraumlösung vor, die platzsparender ist: Ein großer Ausziehschrank, der auf Schienen gleitet, die an der Decke angebracht sind.

Plutôt que de choisir une armoire classique pour la chambre d'enfant, l'équipe de concepteurs a proposé une solution de rangement bien plus efficace et créative sous la forme d'un grand placard escamotable qui coulisse le long de rails attachés au plafond.

En el cuarto de los niños, en lugar de optar por un armario estándar, el equipo de diseño propuso una solución de almacenaje más creativa y eficiente consistente en un gran armario que se desliza por el techo mediante unos rieles.

110 m² // 1,184 sq ft

Photo © Adi Cohen Zedek

WEISEL APARTMENT // DORI INTERIOR DESIGN STUDIO

TEL AVIV, ISRAEL

The remodel of an apartment originally made of a piecemeal of rooms and a long narrow hallway was turned into a bright and spacious home. A storage block is concentrated in the centre of the home, where it doesn't obstruct light and views.

Die Umgestaltung dieser Wohnung, die ursprünglich aus vielen zusammengestückelten Räumen und einem langen schmalen Flur bestand, brachte ein helles und geräumiges Zuhause hervor. Ein Block als Stauraum wird in der Mitte des Hauses platziert, wo er weder den Lichteinfall behindert, noch die Sicht versperrt.

Cet appartement a été totalement réagencé : originellement composé d'un assortiment de pièces et d'un long et étroit couloir, c'est aujourd'hui une habitation lumineuse et spacieuse. Un bloc de rangement a été placé au centre de la maison, à un endroit où il n'obstrue ni la lumière ni la vue.

La remodelación del apartamento —originalmente compuesto por una red de habitaciones y un largo y estrecho pasillo— ha dado lugar a un hogar espacioso e iluminado. En el centro de la casa se ubica un bloque de almacenaje donde no obstruye la luz ni las vistas.

www.dori-design.com // Team: Dori Redlich

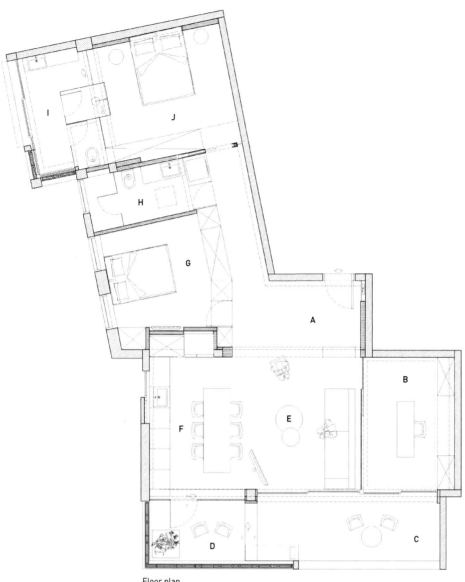

Floor plan

A. Entrance
B. Bedroom/office
C. Terrace
D. Patio
E. Living area
F. Open kitchen
G. Bedroom
H. Bathroom
I. Master bathroom
J. Master bedroom

The design maximizes natural lighting and openness, avoiding obtrusive partitions. Separation of spaces is only used where strictly necessary. In this respect, the need for storage space and for room separation was resolved with one single element.

Die konstruktive Ausführung maximiert die natürliche Beleuchtung und Offenheit und vermeidet zu auffällige Trennwände. Räume werden nur dort abgetrennt, wo es unbedingt notwendig ist. In dieser Hinsicht erfüllt ein einzelnes Element den Bedarf an Stauraum und die nötige Raumtrennung.

Cet agencement optimise la lumière naturelle et privilégie l'ouverture en évitant des cloisons encombrantes. Les espaces sont séparés seulement lorsque cela est nécessaire. De fait, le besoin de rangement et de cloisonnement a été résolu avec un seul module.

El diseño maximiza la luz natural y la amplitud, evitando hacer divisiones molestas. Los espacios solo se separan cuando es necesario. En este sentido, la necesidad de espacio de almacenamiento y de separación de habitaciones se resolvió con un único elemento.

A curtain can be drawn along the glass partition for further separation. This design gesture responds to the desire to keep the separation between areas to a minimum. A minimalistic shelving system delimits the entry hall while allowing visual connection with the living area and through the windows beyond.

Entlang der Glastrennwand kann ein Vorhang als zusätzliche Trennung vorgezogen werden. Diese Gestaltungsgeste reagiert auf den Wunsch, die Trennung zwischen den Bereichen auf ein Minimum zu begrenzen. Ein minimalistisches Regalsystem begrenzt die Eingangshalle und ermöglicht gleichzeitig eine visuelle Verbindung mit dem Wohnbereich und durch die Fenster dahinter.

Le rideau tiré le long de la cloison de verre procure une séparation supplémentaire. Cet élément de la conception répond au désir d'établir une continuité maximale entre les zones. Le système d'étagères minimalistes délimite le vestibule, tout en permettant de regarder à l'intérieur de l'espace de vie et à travers les fenêtres.

Se puede colocar una cortina en la pared de cristal para conseguir una mayor separación del espacio. Esta forma de diseñar responde al deseo de mantener la separación de ambientes, a la mínima expresión. Un sistema minimalista de estanterías delimita el hall de entrada y permite la conexión visual con la sala de estar y con las ventanas del fondo.

Hideaway storage is critical when it comes to keeping a kitchen organised and clean, while open shelving can provide visual appeal.

Versteckter Stauraum ist kritisch, wenn es darum geht, eine Küche aufgeräumt und sauber zu halten, während offene Regale für einen visuellen Reiz sorgen können.

Alors que les étagères peuvent avoir un intérêt visuel, le rangement caché est fondamental pour ce qui est de maintenir organisation et propreté dans la cuisine.

Disponer del espacio de almacenamiento oculto es vital cuando se quiere tener organizada y limpia la cocina, mientras que el sistema de estantes abierto puede resultar atractivo a la vista.

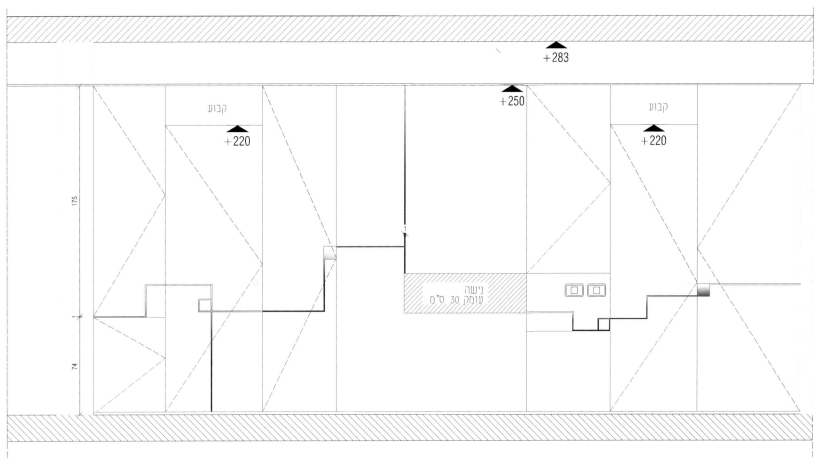

+283

+250

+220

+220

קבוע

קבוע

175

74

נישה
עומק 30 ס"מ

Hallway cabinet elevation

The hallway connecting the living area with the master bedroom offers an opportunity for high-density storage as well as camouflaged access to a bedroom and bathroom behind a continuous wood-panelled wall with black detailing.

Der Korridor, der den Wohnbereich mit dem Hauptschlafzimmer verbindet, bietet eine Möglichkeit für Stauraum mit hoher Dichte sowie einen getarnten Zugang zu einem Schlaf- und Badezimmer hinter einer durchgehenden holzgetäfelten Wand mit Details in Schwarz.

Le couloir qui relie le salon et la chambre parentale est un vaste espace de rangement. L'accès à la chambre et la salle de bain est dissimulé derrière un mur en lambris continu avec des éléments de décoration noirs.

El pasillo que conecta la sala de estar con la habitación principal permite mucho almacenaje. Además, camufla en una pared panelada en madera con detalles en negro el acceso a un dormitorio y a un baño.

30 m² // 323 sq ft

Photo © PION - piondaily.tumblr.com

LONG ESTATE // MILI MŁODZI LUDZIE
POZNAŃ, POLAND

For the remodel of a townhouse's attic, the owners requested a living room with a kitchenette, and a sleeping area with a bathroom. The usable space is optimized despite the irregularity of the walls and ceiling. In fact, these surfaces are a distinctive design element, which provide the space with character.

Bei Umgestaltung des Dachgeschosses dieser Stadtwohnung verlangten die Besitzer ein Wohnzimmer mit einer Kochnische und einen Schlafbereich mit Bad. Die Nutzfläche wird trotz der Unregelmäßigkeit von Wänden und Decke optimiert. Diese Flächen sind sogar zu einem unverwechselbaren Designelement, das dem Raum Charakter verleiht, geworden.

Pour le remaniement du grenier de cette maison de ville, les propriétaires avaient envie d'un salon avec une kitchenette et d'un coin nuit avec salle de bains. L'espace disponible est optimisé malgré l'irrégularité des murs et du plafond. En fait, ces surfaces sont un élément d'agencement distinctif qui contribue à donner du caractère au lieu.

Para la remodelación del ático en una casa adosada, los dueños pidieron una zona de estar con cocina y un dormitorio con baño. El espacio útil se optimiza, a pesar de las irregularidades de las paredes y el techo. De hecho, estas superficies son un elemento de diseño distintivo, que dan carácter al espacio.

www.milimlodziludzie.com // Team: Mili Młodzi Ludzie

The black wall, called "the ribbon", integrates a bathroom that separates the area dedicated to daily activities from the bedroom. The geometry served as inspiration for the design of the kitchenette, the TV unit, and other integrated cabinets.

Die schwarze Wand namens „Band" integriert ein Badezimmer, das den Bereich, der den täglichen Aktivitäten dient, vom Schlafzimmer abtrennt. Die Geometrie fungierte als Inspiration für die Gestaltung der Kochzeile, der TV-Einheit und anderer integrierter Schränke.

Le mur noir, appelé « le ruban », intègre une salle de bains qui sépare l'espace voué aux activités journalières de la chambre. La kitchenette, le bloc TV, et d'autres placards intégrés sont de formes géométriques.

La pared negra, llamada "la cinta", integra el baño y separa la zona dedicada a las actividades diarias del dormitorio. La geometría sirve de inspiración para el diseño de la cocina, el mueble del televisor y otros armarios integrados.

Design development diagrams

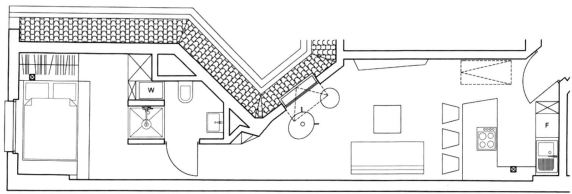

Floor plan

The raised platform bed offers easy-to-reach linen storage. This compact sleeping area would not be complete without various integrated pullout drawers that add convenient storage space.

Das Bett auf einer erhöhten Plattform bietet leicht zugänglichen Stauraum für Bettwäsche. Dieser kompakte Schlafbereich wäre nicht vollständig ohne verschiedene integrierte Ausziehschubladen, die für weiteren praktischen Stauraum sorgen.

Le lit plateforme surélevé offre un rangement facile à atteindre pour le linge de maison. Cette solution de couchage compact ne serait pas complète sans divers tiroirs escamotables intégrés qui ajoutent divers rangements bien pratiques.

La cama, sobre una plataforma elevada, ofrece espacio para guardar la ropa blanca. Esta compacta zona de descanso no estaría completa sin varios cajones extraibles integrados que añaden un espacio de almacenamiento muy útil.

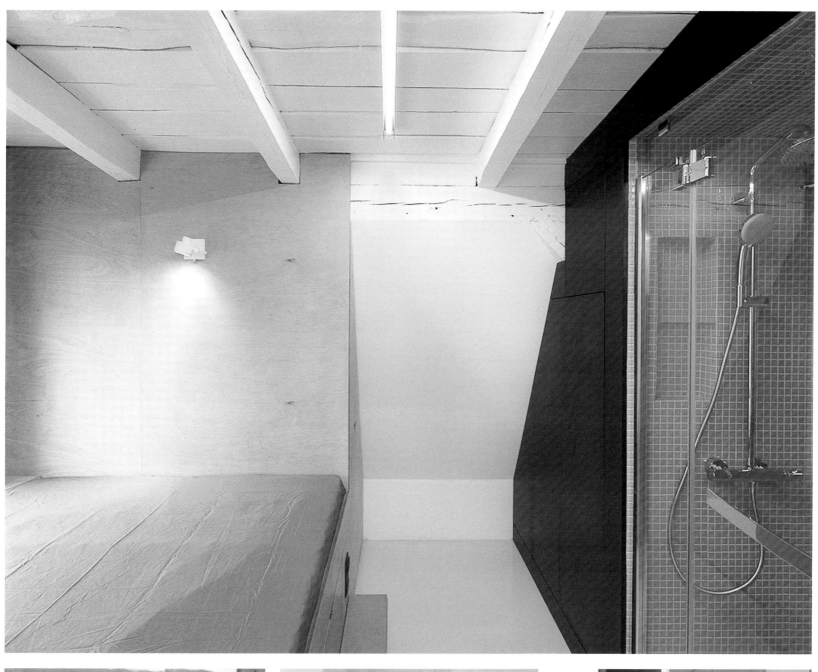

26 m² // 280 sq ft

© Lusia Kosik

PETER'S APARTMENT // MILI MŁODZI LUDZIE

POZNAŃ, POLAND

The surfaces in Peter's Flat are entirely white, from the resin flooring and panelling of the walls and ceiling, to the minimalistic design of the kitchen. This immaculate décor is however disrupted by a series of grooves that trace the configuration of the cabinets.

Die Flächen in Peter's Flat sind vom Harzboden und der Wand- und Deckenverkleidung bis hin zum minimalistischen Design der Küche völlig weiß. Dieses makellose Dekor wird jedoch von einer Reihe von Rillen unterbrochen, welche die Anordnung der Schränke nachzeichnen.

Les surfaces de l'appartement de Peter sont entièrement blanches, du sol au lambris en résine des murs jusqu'au plafond au design minimaliste de la cuisine. Ce décor immaculé est cependant structuré par une série de rainures qui permettent de repérer la configuration des placards.

Las superficies en el Apartamento de Peter son completamente blancas, desde el suelo en resina, los paneles de las paredes y techo al diseño minimalista de la cocina. Este decorado inmaculado es interrumpido, sin embargo, por una serie de ranuras que marcan la configuración de los armarios.

www.milimlodziludzie.com // Team: Mili Młodzi Ludzie

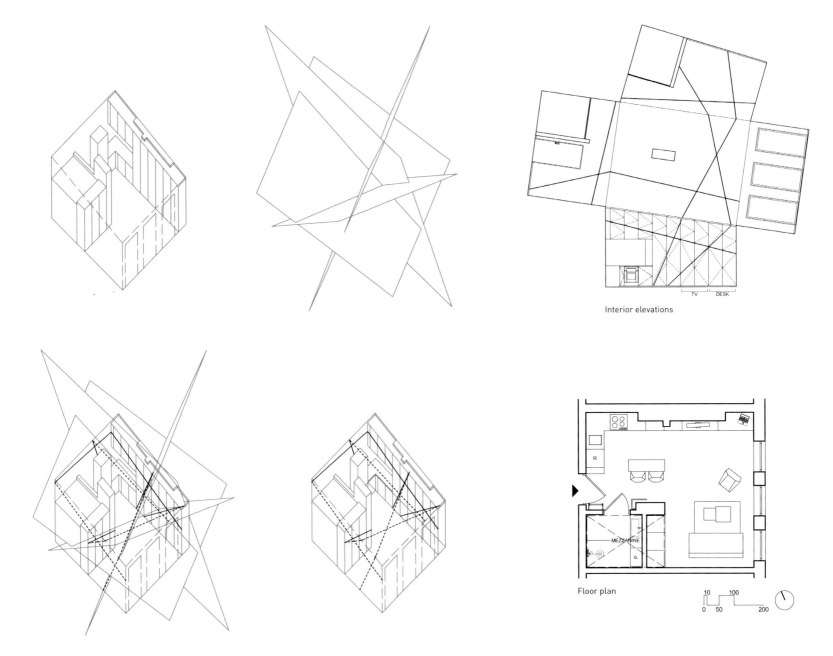

Ideogram

Interior elevations

Floor plan

10 100
0 50   200

The lines crisscrossing the walls and ceiling of the apartment are generated by four imaginary intersecting planes.

Die Linien, welche die Wände und die Decke der Wohnung durchkreuzen, werden durch vier imaginäre Schnittebenen erzeugt.

Les lignes qui sillonnent les murs et le plafond sont dessinées suivant l'idée de quatre avions imaginaires qui se croisent.

Las líneas que se cruzan en las paredes y el techo del apartamento se generan por la conexión de cuatro planos imaginarios.

Some cabinets are full height, while others are short of the ceiling, expanding the perception of the space, already enhanced by the continuous cuts in the walls and ceiling.

Einige Schränke erstrecken sich auf die volle Höhe, während andere knapp an der Decke enden, wodurch die Raumwahrnehmung erweitert wird, die bereits durch durchgehende Schnitte an Wänden und Decke verstärkt wird.

Certains placards ont pleine hauteur, tandis que d'autres s'arrêtent avant le plafond, ce qui accroît le sentiment d'espace, déjà souligné par les rayures continues découpées dans les murs et le plafond.

Algunos armarios van del suelo al techo, mientras que otros no llegan hasta el suelo, aumentando la sensación de amplitud, ya de por si realzada por los cortes constantes en las paredes y el techo.

A loft bed was devised on top of the bathroom. It is accessible by means of a black steel ladder. Its design echoes the dark shadow lines that crisscross the surfaces of the apartment. In terms of functionality, the loft bed is undoubtedly an effective space-saving solution for small homes.

Ein Hochbett wurde oberhalb des Badezimmers geplant und ist über eine schwarze Stahlleiter erreichbar. Das Design gibt die dunklen Schattenlinien wieder, welche die Flächen der Wohnung durchkreuzen. In puncto Funktionalität ist das Hochbett zweifellos eine probate Platzsparlösung für kleine Wohnstätten.

Un lit mezzanine a été installé au-dessus de la salle de bains. Il est accessible par une échelle noire en acier. Son design fait écho aux lignes sombres qui sillonnent les différentes surfaces de l'appartement. En matière de fonctionnalité, ce lit représente sans aucun doute une solution efficace pour les logements de petite taille ayant besoin d'économiser l'espace disponible.

Se diseñó una cama sobre el techo del baño accesible mediante una escalera de acero negro. Su diseño recuerda a las líneas oscuras que cruzan las superficies del apartamento. En términos de funcionalidad, la cama en altura es sin duda una solución efectiva para ahorrar espacio en viviendas pequeñas.

42 m² // 452 sq ft

MY HOME AND OFFICE // SILVIA ALLORI

FLORENCE, ITALY

The renovation of a small 70's apartment was aimed at making the most of the space available without sacrificing comfort. The white on white colour scheme of the apartment seems to have been chosen to disguise its many hidden nooks.

Der Umbau dieser kleinen Wohnung aus den siebziger Jahren zielte darauf ab, das Beste aus dem zur Verfügung stehenden Raum zu machen, ohne Komfort einzubüßen. Das Weiß-auf-Weiß-Farbschema der Wohnung wurde anscheinend gewählt, um ihre vielen versteckten Ecken zu verbergen.

La rénovation de ce petit appartement des années 1970 visait à tirer avantage de l'espace disponible sans sacrifier le confort de vie. Les tons blancs de cet espace semblent avoir été choisis pour en dissimuler les nombreux recoins.

La renovación de un pequeño apartamento de los años 70 tenía como objetivo aprovechar al máximo el espacio disponible sin sacrificar el confort. La elección de una paleta de color de blanco sobre blanco en el apartamento parece camuflar sus muchos rincones ocultos.

www.silviaallori.it // Team: Silvia Allori

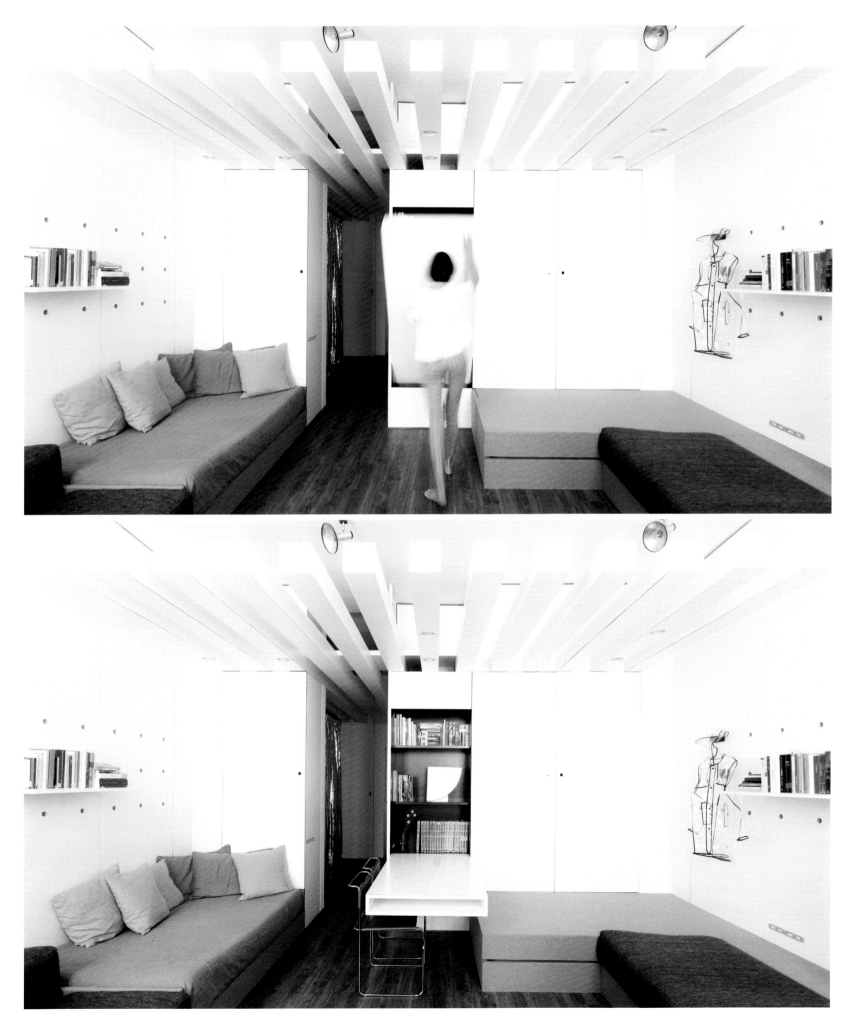

Providing storage space was a programmatic requirement, which was, nonetheless, approached in a playful way. Any conventional ideas regarding open shelving were rejected in favour of a pegboard system that allows for a multitude of configurations.

Die Bereitstellung von Stauraum war eine programmatische Anforderung, die dennoch auf spielerische Art und Weise angegangen wurde. Der Planer lehnte alle herkömmlichen Ideen bezüglich offener Regale zugunsten eines Stecktafelsystems ab, das eine Vielzahl von Anordnungen ermöglicht.

Avoir des espaces de rangement était l'idée directrice de cet aménagement qui s'en est accommodé de manière ludique. Les rayonnages traditionnels ont été écartés en faveur d'un système de panneau perforé qui permet une multitude de configurations.

Uno de los principales requisitos era proporcionar espacio de almacenamiento, el cual fue abordado de una manera lúdica. Se rechazaron las estanterías abiertas convencionales en favor de un sistema mural lleno de pequeños agujeros, que permite infinidad de configuraciones.

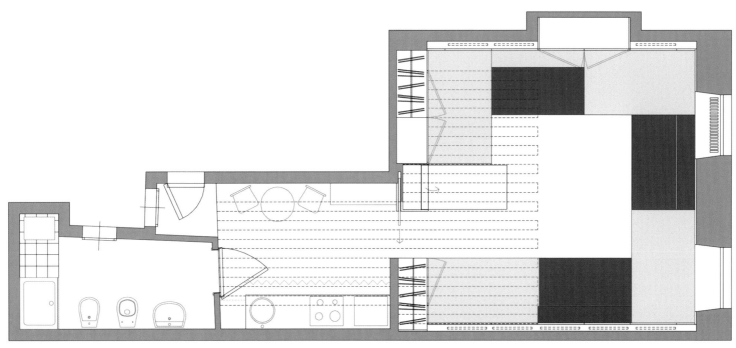

Floor plan

A continuous bench along the four living room walls provides plenty of seating and bedding. Two large closets add thickness to the wall adjacent to the kitchen, allowing for a pocket door to separate the living area from the kitchen and bathroom and for a niche accommodating a foldaway table.

Eine durchgehende Bank entlang der vier Wohnzimmerwände bietet viele Sitzgelegenheiten und Platz für Bettwäsche. Zwei große Wandschränke verleihen der Wand neben der Küche Stärke und schaffen Raum für eine Taschenschiebetür, die den Wohnraum von Küche und Bad abtrennt, und für eine Nische, die einen Klapptisch beherbergt.

Une même banquette suit les quatre murs du salon, procurant beaucoup d'espace pour s'asseoir ou se coucher. Deux grands placards ajoutent de l'épaisseur au mur adjacent à la cuisine, ce qui permet l'existence d'une porte escamotable pour séparer la pièce de vie de la cuisine et de la salle de bains, ainsi que d'une niche pour une table pliante.

Un banco corrido a lo largo de las cuatro paredes del salón proporciona mucho espacio para sentarse y descansar. Dos armarios grandes añaden volumen a la pared que está al lado de la cocina permitiendo una puerta corredera que separa el salón de la cocina y el baño y un pequeño espacio para una mesa plegable.

A golden metallic curtain, made with an isothermal emergency blanket from a survival kit, separates the kitchen from the corridor. It brings colour and sparkle to the all-white scheme, while transforming the kitchen into a sitting area.

Ein goldener Metallvorhang, der aus einer Rettungswärmedecke aus einer Überlebensausrüstung gefertigt ist, trennt die Küche vom Flur. Er bringt Farbe und Glanz in den reinweißen Entwurf und verwandelt die Küche in einen Sitzbereich.

Un rideau métallique doré, créé à partir d'une couverture isotherme issue d'un kit de survie, sépare la cuisine du couloir. Il apporte couleur et brillant à la palette des blancs, tout en transformant la cuisine en coin salon.

Una cortina metálica dorada, realizada con una manta isotérmica de un kit de supervivencia, separa la cocina del pasillo. Aporta color y brillo al diseño del "todo en blanco", a la vez que transforma la cocina en una zona de estar.

96 m² // 1,033 sq ft

EAST COAST APARTMENT // OBLLIQUE

SINGAPORE, SINGAPORE

A 60's apartment offers a surprise when the contemporary interior reveals itself. Two bedrooms were demolished to make room for an airy home. With raw concrete and pale wood finishes as the backdrop, the owner's eclectic collection of vintage items and personal belongings take centre stage, meticulously displayed and organised.

Diese Wohnung aus den sechziger Jahren bietet eine Überraschung, da sich hier das zeitgenössische Interieur zeigt. Zwei Schlafzimmer wurden abgerissen, um Platz für ein luftiges Zuhause zu schaffen. Vor dem Hintergrund des unverputzten Betons und der blassen Holzoberflächenbearbeitungen steht die vielseitige Sammlung des Wohnungsbesitzers im Mittelpunkt, die aus Vintage-Elementen und persönlichen Gegenständen besteht, die sorgfältig ausgestellt und angeordnet sind.

Cet appartement des années 1960 surprend par son intérieur contemporain. Deux chambres ont été démolies pour obtenir un espace ouvert. Avec du béton et des finitions en bois comme toile de fond, la collection éclectique d'objets vintage et les biens personnels du propriétaire sont mis en évidence, exposés et organisés méticuleusement.

Un apartamento de los años 60 resulta sorprendente cuando se desvela su interior contemporáneo. Se demolieron dos habitaciones para conseguir una casa muy amplia. Con acabados en hormigón y madera pálida como telón de fondo, la ecléctica colección de objetos *vintage* y artículos personales del propietario tiene todo el protagonismo, organizada y mostrada de una manera muy meticulosa.

www.obllique.com // Team: Abigael Tay

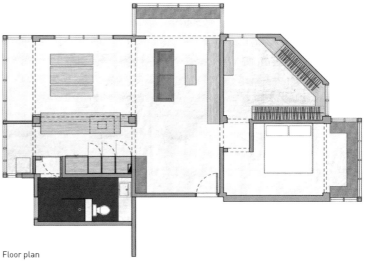

Floor plan

Wardrobe view. Peg board, mirror ands drawer

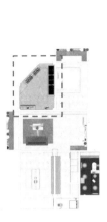

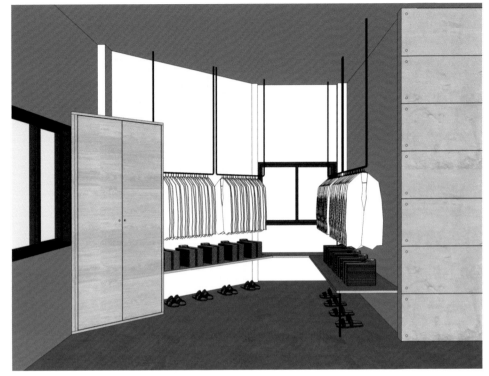

Wardrobe view. Clothes rack and shelf

The walk-in wardrobe is sculptural with clothes racks suspended from the ceiling and wood shelves that seem to float.

Der begehbare Kleiderschrank ähnelt einer Skulptur aus an der Decke aufgehängten Kleiderständern und Holzregalen, die zu schweben scheinen.

Le dressing a un aspect sculptural avec sa penderie suspendue au plafond et ses étagères qui semblent flotter.

El armario vestidor es escultural, con estantes para ropa suspendidos del techo y estanterías de madera que parecen flotar.

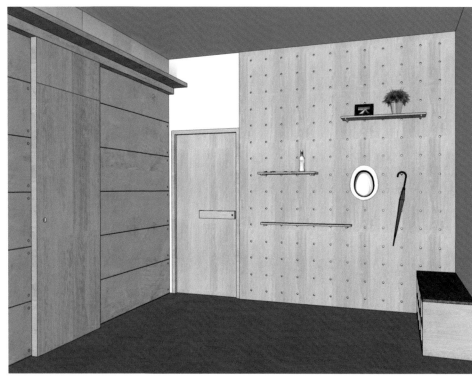
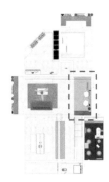

Living room view. Main door, shoe cabinet and peg board wall

A floor-to-ceiling pegboard wall allows for the playful display of items. Shelves and hooks can be placed for an ever-changing wall composition.

Eine raumhohe Stecktafelwand ermöglicht die spielerische Darstellung von Gegenständen. Für einen stetig wechselnden Wandaufbau können Regale und Haken beliebig platziert werden.

Un panneau perforé allant du sol au plafond permet de disposer les objets de façon ludique. Des étagères et des crochets peuvent être placés dessus pour des compositions murales modifiables à l'infini.

Un muro de suelo a techo lleno de pequeños agujeros, deja ver la divertida exposición de objetos. Estanterías y ganchos pueden ser colocados y cambiados como se quiera en esta composición mural.

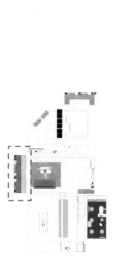

Living room view. Bay window seat

A padded window seat with open storage beneath provides ample storage for books and baskets.

Ein gepolsterter Fenstersitz mit einem offenen Fach darunter bietet reichlich Stauraum für Bücher und Körbe.

Une banquette de fenêtre matelassée au-dessus d'un espace de rangement ouvert offre amplement de quoi ranger livres et chaussures.

Un banco acolchado de ventana deja debajo, espacio abierto de almacenaje para guardar libros y cajas.

Bedroom view. Bay window seat

The window seat in the bedroom is a variation of the one in the living area. Instead of open storage below the seat, it has drawers.

Der Fenstersitz im Schlafzimmer ist eine Variante des Fenstersitzes im Wohnbereich. Statt des offenen Fachs unter dem Sitz hat er jedoch Schubfächer.

La banquette de fenêtre de la chambre est une variante de celle du séjour. Au lieu de rangements ouverts, on y trouve des tiroirs.

El banco de ventana de la habitación es una variante del existente en el salón. En lugar de almacenamiento abierto, tiene cajones bajo el asiento.

76 m² // 818 sq ft

Photo © Kuomin Lee

VIVID COLOR // WATERFROM DESIGN

TAIPEI CITY, CHINA

The design of this apartment takes cue from the fashion world. Fabrics, patterns, templates, colour, and pieces of machinery are reinterpreted in an architectural language to create an original and inspiring home for a fashion designer.

Die Gestaltung dieser Wohnung hat sich von der Modewelt inspirieren lassen. Stoffe, Muster, Vorlagen, Farben und Maschinenteile werden in einer architektonischen Sprache uminterpretiert, um ein originelles und inspirierendes Heim für einen Modedesigner zu schaffen.

L'aménagement de cet appartement s'inspire du monde de la mode. Les tissus, les motifs, les modèles, les couleurs, et la machinerie sont réinterprétés dans un langage architectural pour créer un intérieur original et stimulant pour un designer.

El diseño de este apartamento sigue el ejemplo del mundo de la moda. Tejidos, patrones, plantillas, color y piezas de maquinaria se reinterpretan con un lenguaje arquitectónico para crear el hogar original e inspirador de un diseñador de moda.

www.waterfrom.com // Team: Li Zhixiang, Lv Siting, and Chen Xi

Sewing machine

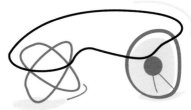

Concept

Dining table

Tools and equipment commonly used in the fashion and clothing industry inspired the design of the furniture and accessories. The dining table is, perhaps, the best example that represents the design team's ability to adapt conceptual ideas to actual products.

Werkzeuge und Ausrüstung, die in der Mode und Bekleidungsindustrie am häufigsten zum Einsatz kommen, regten zur Gestaltung der Möbel und Accessoires an. Der Esstisch ist möglicherweise das beste Beispiel für die Fähigkeit des Designteams, konzeptuelle Ideen an die tatsächlichen Produkte anzupassen.

Pour concevoir le mobilier et les accessoires, les designers se sont inspirés des équipements généralement utilisés dans l'industrie de la mode et de la haute couture. La table de la salle à manger est probablement le meilleur exemple de la capacité de ces créatifs à réaliser leurs idées de manière concrète.

Las herramientas y el equipo normalmente utilizados en la industria de la moda y la confección inspiraron el diseño de los muebles y accesorios. La mesa de comedor es, quizás, el mejor ejemplo de representación de la capacidad del equipo de diseño para adaptar ideas conceptuales a productos reales.

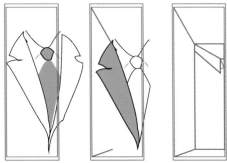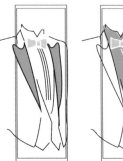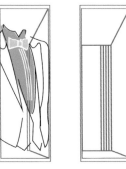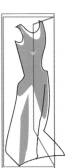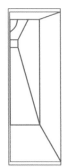

Conceptual design developement for the bookcase

The eye-catching design of the bespoke glass and metal-framed bookcase in the living area evolved from an abstraction process that started with a realistic depiction of two fashion garments, a gown and a tie.

Das ins Auge fallende Design dieses maß-gefertigten Bücherregals aus Glas und Metallrahmen im Wohnbereich entwickelte sich aus einem Abstraktionsprozess, der mit der realistischen Darstellung von zwei Kleidungsstücken, einem Kleid und einer Krawatte, begann.

Le design accrocheur de la bibliothèque du séjour en verre cerclée de métal, conçue sur mesure, est parti d'un processus d'abs-traction né d'une description réaliste de deux vêtements, d'une veste de costume et d'une cravate.

El llamativo diseño de la librería del salón, realizada a medida con vidrio y perfiles de metal, evolucionó a partir de un proceso de abstracción que comenzó con la representa-ción realista de dos prendas de moda, un vestido y una corbata.

The translucent nature of some fabrics has influenced the design of a bookcase in the centre of the house. Made of metallic mesh and glass, the bookcase displays see-through effects and reflections that expand the perception of space.

Die lichtdurchlässige Natur einiger Gewebe hat das Design eines Bücherregals in der Mitte des Hauses beeinflusst. Aus Metallnetz und Glas gefertigt, weist das Bücherregal Durchsichteffekte und Reflexionen auf, welche die Raumwahrnehmung erweitern.

La nature translucide de certains tissus a influencé le design d'une bibliothèque positionnée au cœur de la maison. Faite de maille métallique et de verre, celle-ci occasionne des effets de transparence et de réflexion qui accroissent la perception de l'espace.

La naturaleza translúcida de algunos tejidos ha influido en el diseño de la librería ubicada en el centro de la casa. Fabricada en rejilla metálica y vidrio, la librería muestra efectos transparentes y reflejos que amplían la percepción del espacio.

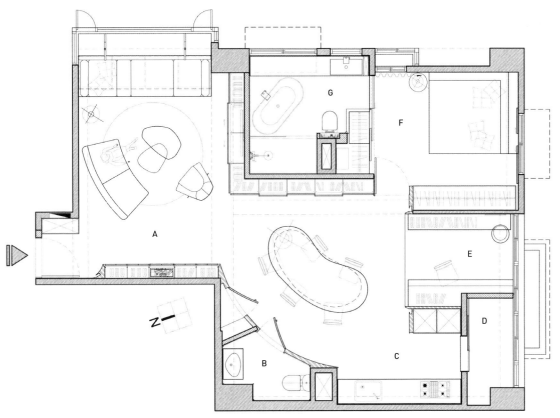

Floor plan

A. Living room   E. Working area
B. Powder room   F. Bedroom
C. Kitchen   G. Bathroom
D. Balcony

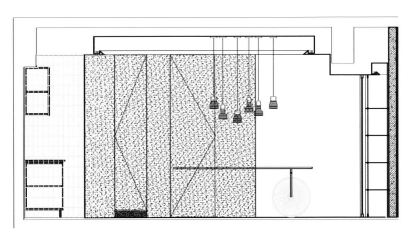

Dining room elevation

Splashes of colour animate the geometric configuration of spaces and the design of furniture.

Farbspritzer beleben die geometrische Gestaltung der Räume und das Design der Wohnungseinrichtung.

Des touches de couleur animent la configuration géométrique des espaces et le design du mobilier.

Toques de color dan vida a la configuración geométrica de los espacios y el diseño de los muebles.

Photo © Rasmus Norlander

PINORAMA // INGA SEMPÉ

www.ingasempe.fr

Pinorama is a modular pin board that includes metal and cork shelves, mirrors and penholders. All the items can be combined, playing with composition and colour. Pinorama offers fun and versatile storage solutions for small items that are often hard to find a place for but need at hand on a daily basis.

Pinorama ist eine modulare Pinnwand, die Metall- und Korkregale, Spiegel und Stifthalter umfasst. Alle Einzelteile können kombiniert werden und spielen mit Komposition und Farbe. Pinorama bietet witzige und vielseitige Lösungen für die Aufbewahrung von Kleinteilen, für die sich häufig schwer ein Platz finden lässt, die im Alltag jedoch zur Hand sein müssen.

Pinorama est un panneau mural modulaire qui comprend des éléments en métal et en liège : étagères, miroirs et porte-crayons. Les différentes combinaisons de ces éléments jouent avec la composition et la couleur. Pinorama est un système de rangement polyvalent et utile pour les petits objets du quotidien qui ont souvent du mal à trouver leur place et qui doivent rester à portée de main.

Pinorama es un tablero modular con estantes de metal y corcho, espejos y portalápices. Todo se puede combinar, jugando con la composición y el color. Pinorama ofrece soluciones de almacenamiento versátiles y divertidas para cosas pequeñas que a menudo no sabemos dónde poner pero que necesitamos tener a mano diariamente.

Manufacturer: HAY // www.hay.dk
Materials: Steel and cork

Design development sketches

Dimension: Small W37 X H50 X D5 cm / Large W68 X H83 X D5 cm
Colors: Light blue (S) Mustard (S) Wine (S) Cream (L) Dark blue (L)

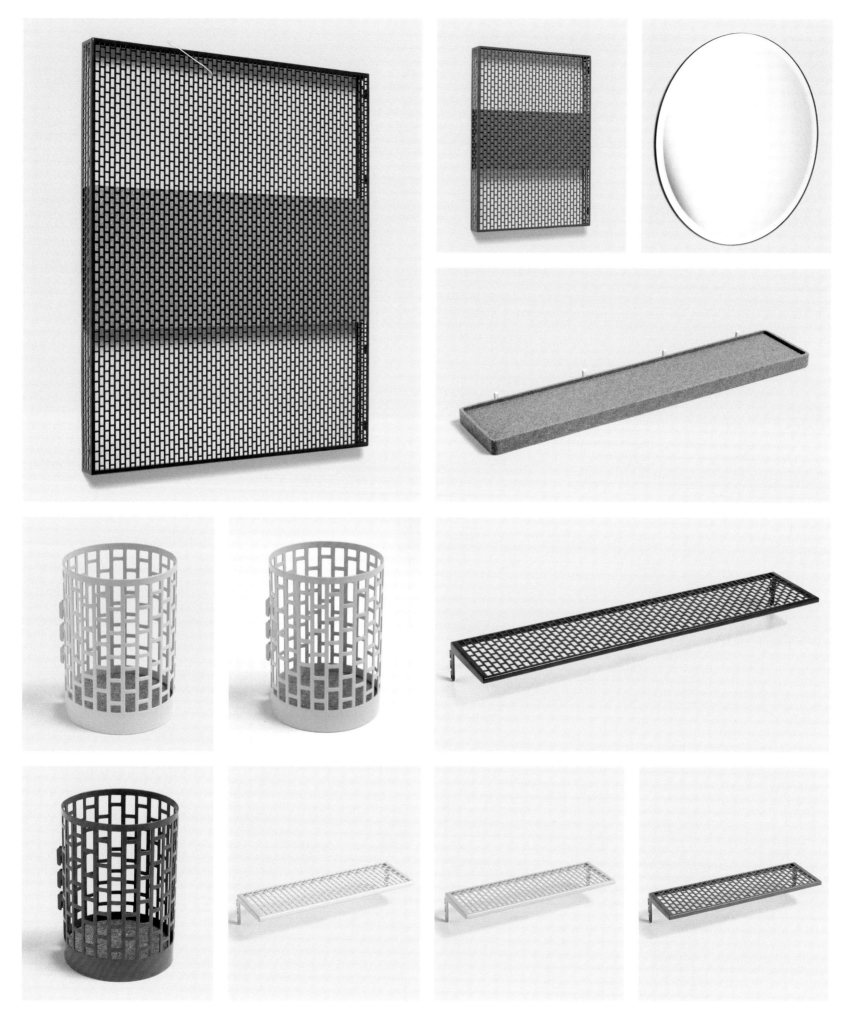

64 m² // 689 sq ft

Photo © Toshiyuki Yano

M HOUSE // SINATO ARCHITECTS

KANAGAWA, JAPAN

The renovation of a small apartment was aimed at creating a living space as open as possible, but with various areas of different functions. The solution was an L-shape wooden wall that generates different areas while maintaining the open character of the apartment, and at the same time, offering various storage and seating solutions.

Die Renovierung dieser kleinen Wohnung war darauf ausgerichtet, einen Lebensraum zu schaffen, der so offen wie möglich ist, bei dem die unterschiedlichen Funktionen jedoch in verschiedenen Bereichen liegen. Die Lösung war eine Holzwand in L-Form, die für unterschiedliche Bereiche sorgt, so dass der offene Charakter der Wohnung beibehalten wird und gleichzeitig verschiedenen Ablagelösungen und Sitzmöglichkeiten bietet.

La rénovation de l'appartement avait pour objectif de créer un espace de vie le plus aéré possible, mais avec différents espaces correspondant à diverses fonctions. Le mur en bois en forme de L permet de créer différents espaces tout en conservant le caractère ouvert de l'appartement. Il offre également une multitude d'endroits pour ranger et s'asseoir.

La renovación del pequeño apartamento tenía como objetivo crear un espacio lo más abierto posible, pero con diversas áreas funcionales. La solución fue una pared de madera en forma de L que crea diferentes estancias que, al mismo tiempo, permite mantener el carácter abierto del apartamento con espacios de almacenaje y reposo.

www.sinato.jp // Team: Chikara Ohno

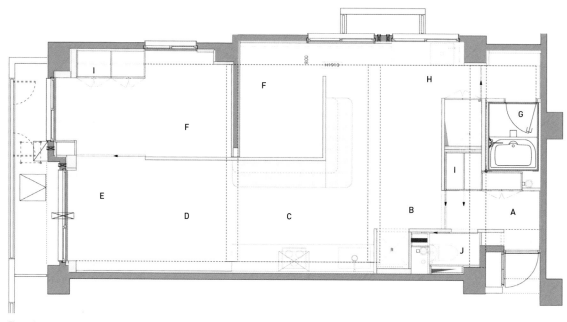

Floor plan

A. Entry
B. Living area
C. Kitchen
D. Dining area
E. Area for relaxation

F. Bedroom
G. Bathroom
H. Washroom
I. Storage
J. Toilet room

The L-shape wooden wall is conceived as a multifunctional large piece of furniture. As such, it is separate from the pre-existing concrete and plaster shell of the apartment. Because of its central position, its surfaces provide each of the areas around it with the required storage and seating requisites.

Diese Holzwand in L-Form wurde als großes multifunktionelles Möbelstück konzipiert. Als solches ist es von der bereits bestehenden Beton- und Putzhülle der Wohnung getrennt. Wegen seiner zentralen Position versehen seine Oberflächen die umliegenden Bereiche mit den erforderlichen Speicher- und Sitzmöglichkeiten.

Le mur en bois en forme de L est conçu comme un grand meuble multifonction. Il est donc indépendant de l'enveloppe en plâtre et béton de l'appartement préexistante. Du fait de leur position centrale, ses surfaces accessibles depuis chacune des zones environnantes offrent les espaces nécessaires pour le rangement ou s'asseoir.

La pared de madera en forma de L se concibe como un gran mueble multifuncional. Es independiente de la carcasa de hormigón y yeso que ya existía en la vivienda. Dada la posición central de la pared, sus superficies proporcionan los requisitos de almacenamiento y reposo que se pretendían en todas las estancias que la rodean.

Perspective view

Additional pieces of furniture along the perimeter of the apartment offer the specific support for each of the functions of the household, as the kitchen cooking area and the vanity.

Zusätzliche Möbelstücke entlang der Umfangslinie der Wohnung bieten die spezifische Unterstützung für alle Funktionen im Haushalt, wie der Kochbereich in der Küche und der Schminktisch.

Le long du périmètre de l'appartement, d'autres éléments du mobilier offrent des systèmes spécifiques pour chacune des fonctions de la maison telle que l'espace cuisson dans la cuisine ou la coiffeuse.

Los muebles adicionales colocados a lo largo del perímetro del apartamento sirven de apoyo a cada una de las funciones propias del hogar, como son la zona de cocinar y el tocador.

48 m² // 416 sq ft

Photo © Ruetemple and NTV Broadcasting Company

LIVING SPACE // RUETEMPLE

MOSCOW, RUSIA

A multifunctional space was devised as an environment where one can either socialize or enjoy the space as a personal retreat. For the latter option, a meditation pod is the heart of the space. The pod is suspended from the ceiling. Conceptually, it infuses the space with spiritual charge; functionally, it frees up floor space.

Ein Multifunktionsraum wurde als Umfeld geplant, in dem der Bewohner entweder Freunde treffen oder den Raum als persönlichen Rückzugsort genießen kann. Für letztere Option bildet eine Meditationskapsel das Herz des Raumes. Die Kapsel ist an der Decke aufgehängt. Konzeptionell verleiht sie dem Raum spirituelle Fülle, funktionell sorgt sie für mehr Nutzfläche.

Cet espace multifonctionnel a été conçu comme un lieu dans lequel on peut aussi bien recevoir des amis que s'isoler pour moment de relaxation. À cet effet, un îlot de méditation est au cœur de cet espace. Suspendu au plafond, celui-ci confère une intensité spirituelle au lieu tout en libérant de la surface au sol.

Este espacio multifuncional fue concebido para crear un ambiente donde se puede socializar o disfrutar como si de un lugar de retiro personal se tratara. En este sentido, el corazón del espacio lo ocupa una cápsula de meditación. La cápsula está suspendida del techo. Conceptualmente, aporta una carga espiritual a la estancia; funcionalmente, libera espacio del suelo.

www.ruetemple.ru // Team: Alexander Kudimov, Daria Butakhina, and Evgeny Dagaev

Tucked into a corner of the space, a large closet offers all the necessary storage. With no kitchen, no bathroom and no proper bedroom, the need for storage is minimized and simplified.

In einer Ecke des Raumes verborgen, bietet ein großer Wandschrank den nötigen Stauraum. Ohne Küche, ohne Bad und ohne richtiges Schlafzimmer wird der Bedarf an Stauraum minimiert und vereinfacht.

Glissé dans un recoin, un grand placard fournit tout le rangement nécessaire. Sans cuisine ni salle de bains, ni véritable chambre, le besoin de rangement est réduit à son minimum.

Ubicado en una esquina del espacio, un gran armario ofrece todo el almacenamiento necesario. La necesidad de almacenamiento se minimiza y simplifica al no disponer de cocina, ni baño ni dormitorio como tal.

Cross section

Longitudinal section

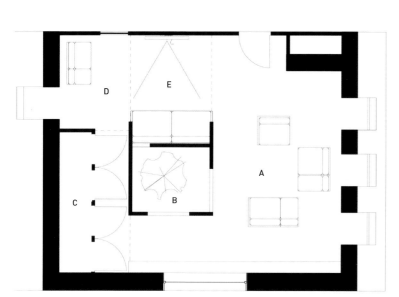

Floor plan

A. Living area
B. Relaxation area
C. Storage
D. Lounge
E. TV area

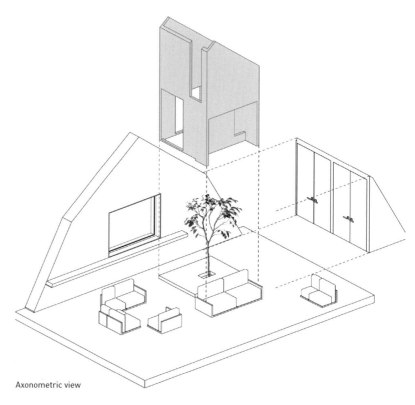

Axonometric view

The space under the pod is used for the storage of a two-tier step ladder to access the meditation pod, three padded benches that can be rolled out to create a sitting area, and a larger bench that doubles as a single bed.

Der Raum unter der Kapsel wird zum Aufbewahren einer zweistufigen Trittleiter verwendet, diese ermöglicht den Zugang zur Meditationskapsel, zu drei gepolsterten Bänken, die ausgerollt werden können, um eine Sitzecke zu schaffen, und zu einer größeren Bank, die auch als Einzelbett dient.

Un petit escabeau permettant d'accéder à l'espace de méditation est rangé sous l'îlot, ainsi que trois banquettes matelassées pouvant être agencées afin de créer un salon ou une banquette plus grande utilisable comme lit simple.

El espacio que está debajo de la cápsula se utiliza para guardar una escalera de dos peldaños y así acceder a la cápsula de meditación, tres bancos acolchados que se pueden deslizar para crear una zona de descanso y un banco más grande que se convierte en una cama individual.

41 m² // 441 sq ft

MOORMANN'S KAMMERSPIEL // NILS HOLGER MOORMANN AND B&O GROUP
PROTOTYPE

In his Kammerspiel —intimate theatre—, the architect has playfully addressed the subject of "living in a small space" with one single large piece of furniture as a centrepiece. This piece of furniture, shaped like a cube, concentrates various household functions to maximise the openness of the space around it.

In seinem Kammerspiel sprach der Architekt das Thema „auf wenig Raum leben" mit einem einzelnen großen Möbelstück als Mittelstück spielerisch an. Dieses wie ein Würfel geformte Möbelstück konzentriert verschiedene Funktionen im Haushalt, um die Offenheit des Raumes darum herum zu maximieren.

Dans ce Kammerspiel – théâtre de chambre – l'architecte a traité de façon ludique sur le sujet « vivre dans un espace limité » avec comme pièce maîtresse un seul meuble de grande taille. Ce meuble, en forme de cube, cumule différentes fonctions domestiques pour faciliter la circulation dans l'espace qui l'entoure.

Kammerspiel —teatro íntimo— ha sido la lúdica respuesta del arquitecto al abordar el tema "vivir en un espacio pequeño". Para ello, ha usado una única pieza de mobiliario de grandes proporciones como eje central. Este mueble, de forma cúbica, alberga varias de las funciones necesarias en un hogar, con el objetivo de maximizar el espacio abierto a su alrededor.

www.moormann.de // Team: Nils Holger Moormann

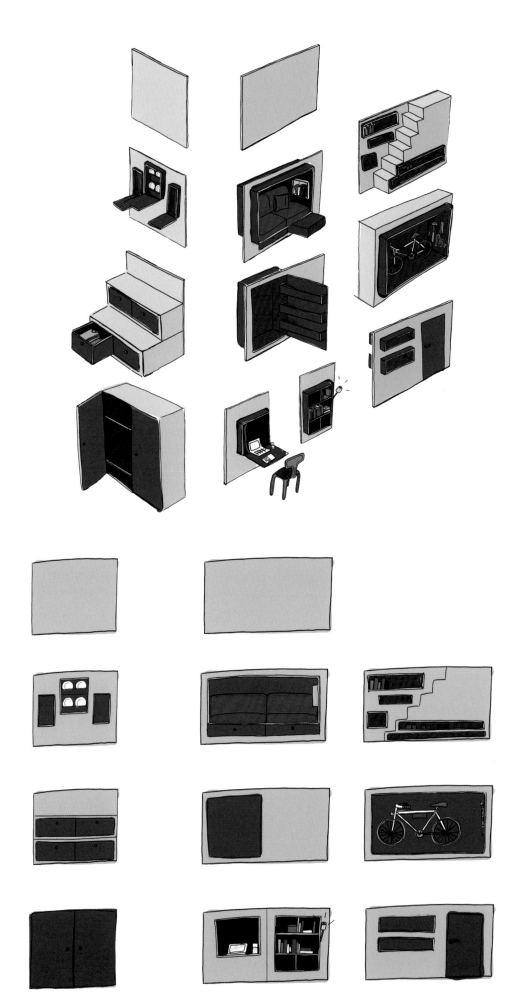

Most domestic functions find their own specific place in the cube. Sleeping, eating, working and reading are organized on the exterior sides, while everyday essentials as well as a walk-in wardrobe have their place in the interior.

Im Würfel haben die meisten häuslichen Funktionen ihren eigenen besonderen Platz. Zum Schlafen, Essen, Arbeiten und Lesen sind die Außenseiten vorgesehen, während die wesentlichen Punkte des Alltags sowie ein begehbarer Kleiderschrank ihren Platz im Innenraum haben.

La plupart des fonctions domestiques trouvent leur place spécifique dans ce cube. Le couchage, les repas et le travail s'organisent sur les côtés extérieurs, tandis que les éléments fondamentaux du quotidien, ainsi qu'un dressing, trouvent leur place à l'intérieur.

La mayoría de las funciones domésticas tienen su lugar específico en el mueble cúbico. Las áreas para dormir, comer, trabajar y leer están organizadas en los lados exteriores, mientras que objetos esenciales diarios y un armario vestidor se albergan en el interior.

Design development sketches

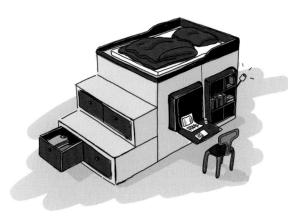

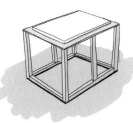

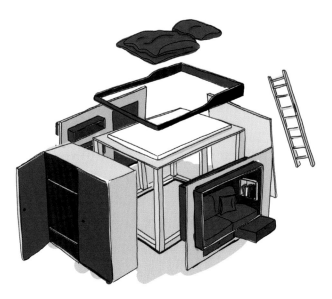

The interior offers storage space for 3 drink crates, 25 wine bottles, a vacuum cleaner, and a cleaning bucket. There is also room for three compartments to keep cleaning supplies, a wall bracket for a snowboard or skis with shelf for shoes and helmet; rails for 6 plastic boxes and a clothes rack.

Das Innere bietet Stauraum für 3 Getränke-kästen, 25 Weinflaschen, einen Staubsauger und einen Putzeimer. Zudem gibt es dort Platz für drei Fächer zum Aufbewahren von Reinigungsutensilien, eine Wandhalterung für ein Snowboard oder Skier mit einem Regal für Schuhe und Helm, Schienen für 6 Plastikkästen und einen Kleiderständer.

L'intérieur contient assez d'espace de ran-gement pour 3 caisses de boissons, 25 bou-teilles de vin, un aspirateur et un seau de ménage. Il y a également de la place pour trois compartiments pouvant contenir du matériel d'entretien, un support mural pour un snowboard ou des skis avec une étagère pour chaussures et casque, des rails destinés à 6 boîtes en plastique et un portemanteau.

El interior contiene espacio para tres bote-lleros, 25 botellas de vino, un aspirador y un cubo. También hay tres compartimentos para guardar productos de limpieza, un soporte de pared para una tabla de *snow* o unos esquís con estante para zapatos y cas-co; raíles para seis botellas de plástico y un estante para ropa.

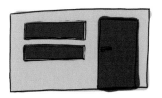

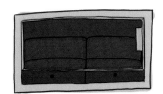

Design development sketches

Floor plan

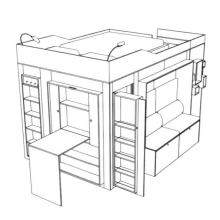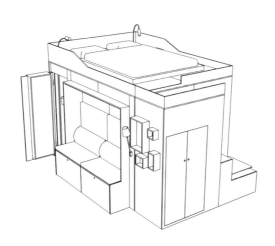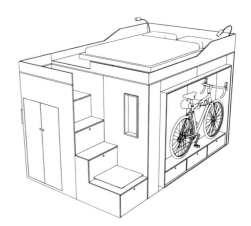

Axonometric views

The composition of the cube can be customized adapting to the lifestyle and habits of the user.

Der Aufbau des Würfels kann individuell an den Lebensstil und die Gewohnheiten der Benutzer angepasst werden.

La composition du cube peut être customisée selon le style de vie et les habitudes de l'usager.

La composición del cubo puede personalizarse adaptándola a la forma de vida y hábitos del usuario.

101 m² // 1,087 sq ft

Photo © Rory Gardiner

ISLINGTON MAISONETTE // LARISSA JOHNSTON ARCHITECTS
LONDON, UNITED KINGDOM

A two-storey Victorian maisonette was reconfigured and extended to create a spacious, bright, and modern family home. This was achieved by locating most utilitarian rooms such the kitchen, powder room, and storage space in a single structure, which, at the same time, connects the two floors.

Eine zweistöckige, viktorianische Maisonette-Wohnung wurde neu konfiguriert und erweitert, um ein geräumiges, helles und modernes Familienheim zu schaffen. Dies wurde erzielt, indem man die meisten Nutzräume wie Küche, Badezimmer und Speicherplatz in einer einzelnen Struktur, die gleichzeitig die beiden Etagen verbindet, unterbrachte.

La maisonnette victorienne à deux niveaux a été reconfigurée et agrandie pour créer une maison familiale spacieuse, lumineuse et moderne. Pour y parvenir, les salles les plus utiles telles que la cuisine, la salle d'eau et l'espace de rangement sont réunies dans une structure unique qui, parallèlement, relie les deux étages.

Esta vivienda victoriana de dos plantas fue reconfigurada y ampliada para crear una casa familiar espaciosa, luminosa y moderna. Se consiguió ubicando las estancias más funcionales como la cocina, el aseo y espacio de almacenamiento en una única estructura que, a su vez, conecta las dos plantas.

www.larissajohnston.com // Team: Larissa Johnston

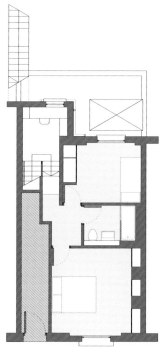

Upper floor plan

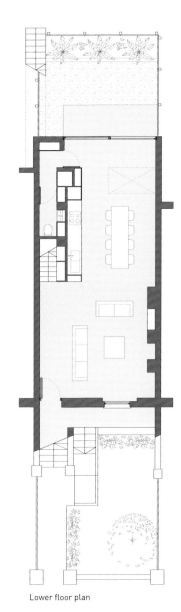

Lower floor plan

At the lower level, all of the existing internal partitions were removed to create an un-interrupted open space. The rear external wall was also removed, allowing an extension to be integrated into the main space.

In der unteren Etage wurden alle bestehenden Trennwände im Innenraum entfernt, um einen durchgehenden offenen Raum zu schaffen. Die hintere Außenwand wurde ebenfalls entfernt, wodurch eine Erweiterung in den Hauptraum integriert werden konnte.

Au niveau inférieur, toutes les partitions internes existantes ont été supprimées pour créer un espace ouvert et continu. Le mur extérieur arrière a également été rasé afin d'intégrer une extension dans l'espace principal.

En la planta baja, se eliminaron todas las divisiones internas existentes para crear un espacio abierto ininterrumpido. La pared externa trasera también se suprimió, dando lugar a una ampliación que se integra con el espacio principal.

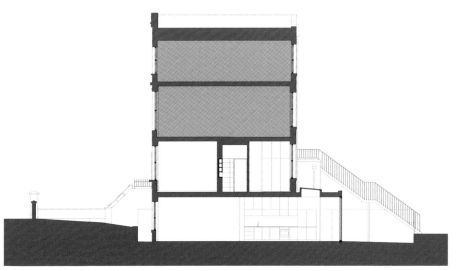

Building section

Inserted within the large space is a compact and efficient plywood "box", which incorporates a fully fitted kitchen, a staircase, a desk with adjacent shelving, and plenty of storage space. A utility room and cloakroom are neatly tucked beneath the stairs.

In den großen Raum eingesetzt ist ein kompakter und effizienter Furnierholz-„Kasten", der eine komplett ausgestattete Küche, die Treppe, einen Schreibtisch mit angrenzendem Regal und viel Speicherplatz enthält. Ein Hauswirtschaftsraum und eine Garderobe sind ordentlich unter der Treppe untergebracht.

Une coquille compacte et performante en contreplaqué est insérée dans ce grand espace et inclut une cuisine entièrement équipée, un escalier, un bureau avec des étagères à proximité et un vaste espace de rangement. Une buanderie et un vestiaire sont ingénieusement nichés sous les escaliers.

En el espacio principal destaca una "caja" compacta de madera contrachapada que incorpora una cocina totalmente equipada, una escalera, un escritorio con estantes adyacentes y un sinfín de espacio de almacenaje. El aseo y el lavadero están cuidadosamente emplazados debajo de la escalera.

The plywood box makes for a strong design statement. It can be understood as an inserted object into the existing building shell, making a clear distinction between what is original and what is new.

Der Sperrholzkasten sorgt für eine überzeugende Designaussage. Er kann als eingesetzter Gegenstand in die bestehende Rohbaustruktur verstanden werden und dadurch deutlich zwischen Ursprünglichem und Neuem unterscheiden.

Le module en contreplaqué est une déclaration d'intention forte. Il peut être considéré comme un objet inséré dans l'architecture du bâtiment d'origine, faisant une distinction claire entre ce qui est d'origine et ce qui est nouveau.

La caja de madera contrachapada supone toda una declaración de diseño. Puede entenderse como un objeto introducido dentro de la construcción ya existente, haciendo una clara distinción entre lo original y lo nuevo.

By concentrating various functions into the box, the need for additional freestanding furniture is minimized. But most importantly, the ground floor is an open area, allowing for a flexible use of the space.

Durch die Konzentration verschiedener Funktionen in den Kästen wird der Bedarf an zusätzlichen freistehenden Möbeln vermindert. Am wichtigsten jedoch ist, dass das Erdgeschoss ein offener Bereich ist und dadurch eine flexible Nutzung des Raumes ermöglicht.

En concentrant diverses fonctions dans ce module, les usagers avaient moins besoin de meubles indépendants. Mais surtout, le rez-de-chaussée reste un espace ouvert, ce qui permet un usage flexible du lieu.

Al concentrar varias funciones dentro de la caja, se minimiza la necesidad de mobiliario adicional independiente. Y aún más importante, convierte la planta baja en una zona abierta, que permite un uso flexible del espacio.

Photo © Hierve Design

VITRINA COLLECTION AND WARDROBE SYSTEM // HIERVE DESIGN

www.hierve.com

Both Vitrina Collection and Wardrobe System put a contemporary spin on classic pieces of furniture, fusing traditional and current design references. The designs take on a bright, distinctive character, inviting people to display their objects and clothes in a playful, yet effective way.

Sowohl Vitrina Collection als auch Wardrobe System geben klassischen Möbelstücken einen modernen Touch, indem sie traditionelle und aktuelle Designelemente verbinden. Die Entwürfe nehmen einen hellen, unverwechselbaren Charakter an und laden die Menschen dazu ein, ihre Gegenstände und Kleidung auf spielerische und dennoch wirkungsvolle Weise zur Schau zu stellen.

Vitrina Collection et Wardrobe System donnent une touche moderne aux éléments classiques du mobilier, en fusionnant concepts traditionnels et références actuelles. Tout en restant efficaces, ces créations confèrent une personnalité particulière et vivante au lieu, en invitant les personnes à montrer leurs objets et vêtements de manière ludique.

Tanto Vitrina Collection como Wardrobe System le dan un toque contemporáneo a piezas de mobiliario clásico, fusionando las referencias de diseño tradicionales con las actuales. Estos diseños atractivos y únicos, nos invitan a mostrar objetos y prendas de una forma lúdica y efectiva.

Manufacturer: Case Furniture // www.casefurniture.com
Materials: exterior: natural solid oak, reinforced 4 mm glass, brushed brass hinges; interior: painted MDF.

The products were designed as visually light and transparent pieces of furniture, providing a wide range of volumetric plays, colour combinations, and lighting effects and reflections.

Die Produkte wurden als optisch leichte und transparente Möbelstücke entworfen, die eine breite Palette an Volumenspielen, Farbkombinationen und Lichteffekten und Reflexionen bieten.

Les meubles ont été conçus avec légèreté et transparence, offrant ainsi une gamme élargie de jeux volumétriques, combinaisons de couleurs et effets de lumière et de reflets.

Los productos fueron diseñados como muebles visualmente ligeros y transparentes, que proporcionan una amplia gama de juegos volumétricos, combinaciones de color y efectos de iluminación y reflejos.

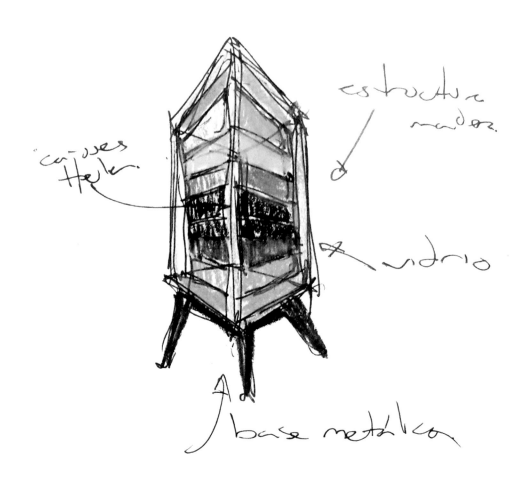

Conceptual design sketch

332

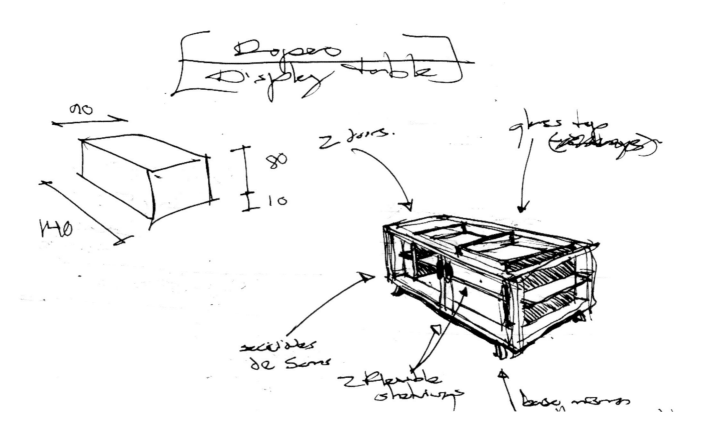

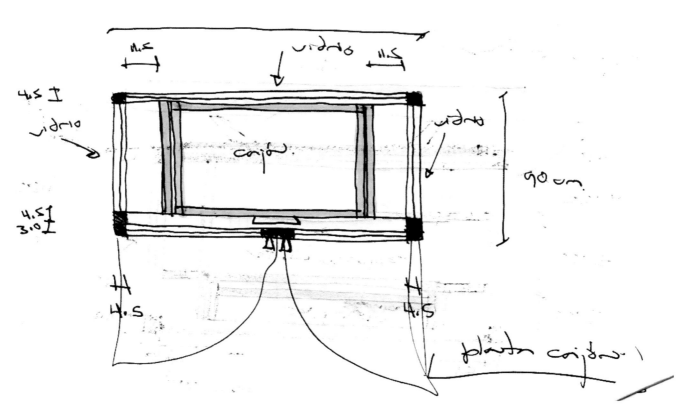

Conceptual design sketches

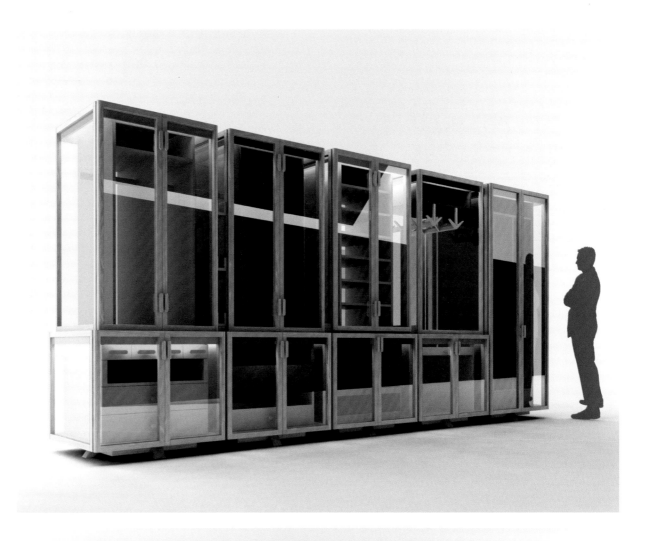

The system consists of a series of modules that offer many arrangement possibilities, and therefore, provide flexibility in use to satisfy storage needs and adapt to space constraints.

Das System besteht aus einer Reihe von Modulen, die viele Anordnungsmöglichkeiten und folglich die Flexibilität bietet, die eingesetzt wird, um den Bedarf an Stauraum zu erfüllen und sich an Raumbegrenzungen anzupassen.

Le système, composé d'une série de modules, offre de nombreuses possibilités d'agencement et permet une souplesse d'utilisation qui répond aux besoins de rangement adaptés aux contraintes d'espace.

El sistema se compone de una serie de módulos que ofrecen muchas posibilidades de organización, y por tanto, de gran flexibilidad en su uso, de cara a satisfacer las necesidades de almacenamiento y adaptándose a las limitaciones de espacio.